GAMBIT PLAY

sacrificing in the opening

Angus Dunnington

EVERYMAN CHESS

Gloucester Publishers plc   www.everymanchess.com

First published in 2003 by Gloucester Publishers plc (formerly Everyman Publishers plc), Gloucester Mansions, 140A Shaftesbury Avenue, London WC2H 8HD

British Library Cataloguing-in-Publication Data
A catalogue record for this book is available from the British Library.

ISBN 1 85744 334 9

Distributed in North America by The Globe Pequot Press, P.O Box 480, 246 Goose Lane, Guilford, CT 06437-0480.

All other sales enquiries should be directed to Everyman Chess, Gloucester Publishers plc, Gloucester Mansions, 140A Shaftesbury Avenue, London WC2H 8HD
tel: 020 7539 7600 fax: 020 7379 4060
email: info@everymanchess.com
website: www.everymanchess.com

EVERYMAN CHESS SERIES (formerly Cadogan Chess)
Chief advisor: Garry Kasparov
Commissioning editor: Byron Jacobs

Typeset and edited by First Rank Publishing, Brighton.
Cover design by Horatio Monteverde.
Production by Navigator Guides.
Printed and bound in Great Britain by Biddles Ltd.

CONTENTS

INTRODUCTION

In an ideal world players could see the bigger picture and avoid getting themselves tied up in order to 'secure' what is essentially a gambit pawn (or pawns) that will come into play much later in the game. But in reality their eyes are too big, they grow attached to gambit pawns and start to break rules that are usually taken for granted. 'Home' squares are neglected, lines open up for the exclusive use of the opposition, pieces – when finally brought into the game, often much later than the enemy forces – end up on unconventional, poor outposts. A good appreciation of this human nature aspect of chess is best exploited by injecting some energy into our play, by keeping a more open mind as to the gambit possibilities that lurk – not too well hidden – in the background of every game.

Every player should be able to make use of such a subtle strategic weapon as a pawn sacrifice – Karpov

Quite simply, this book aims to attract the reader to the idea of playing gambits, of sacrificing a pawn or two (or three...) in the early stages of the game in return for a development advantage, open lines or an influential knight outpost, for example. The practical examples in this book are biased in favour of the gambit and its many uses, as these pages have been designed to offer a taste of a key part of the game rather than a foolproof, watertight weapon.

Chess should not be easy, but it should be fun, and my intention when annotating these games was to put together a collection of gambit oriented lessons that provide an interesting and instructive guide to your next destination on the road to chess discovery.

It is imperative that a gambit has an agenda, that parting with a pawn or more is an investment for the near or not so near future, a price to pay in return for some other, non-material factor(s). Anything else, any offer that is really conditional on the opposition blundering or playing poor moves, then this is not a proper gambit, rather a gift, and we are not in the business of giving something for nothing when we sit down to play...

Incidentally, while I am happy to recommend that you play through the gambit displays of worthy role models such as Kramnik and Spassky with a view to emulating their exploits, any theoretical opinions in these pages should not be used as the foundations of an opening repertoire. While I have tried in some of the more heavily annotated games to provide a certain level of help on the subject, this is not a theoretical openings book. However, a few of the lines seem quite interesting from a would-be gambiteer's point of view, and I have (carefully) made a few hints where appropriate, but don't forget that the success of gambit play often boils down to practical, psychological factors...

And remember – Gambits are Fun.

CHAPTER ONE

Time

When weighing up the various factors that determine the flavour of a game, time and development tend to be overlooked, and to a dangerous degree – particularly among club players. We know that a knight is worth approximately three pawns, that two rooks are a match for a queen and so on, but this is judging like for like. When the value of a pawn is measured against time, however, confusion sets in.

Those players for whom pawns barely register as actual pieces, as loyal foot soldiers that might well win the game, think nothing of letting them go for practically no compensation. Yet these players – ironically – will have more interesting games and are sufficiently uninhibited to cause their opponents problems. Of course they are more likely than the rest of us to find themselves on the wrong side of difficult rook endings, but at least it is easier to make a conscious effort to devote a little more care when contemplating gambits than it is to adopt a new and more versatile approach to the game. In this chapter we will look at a few sim-ple, traditional examples of one side putting his faith in points, the other in time. In the first game White seems to create problems for himself by allowing the displacement of his king, but the strategy is to exploit the predicament of the enemy king.

Kramnik-Kaidanov
Groningen 1993

1 ♘f3 d5 2 d4 ♘f6 3 c4 e6 4 ♘c3 dxc4 5 e4 ♝b4 6 ♝g5 c5

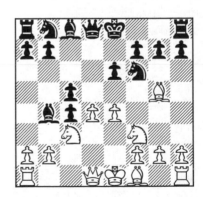

You should gather from the diagram position that the Vienna Variation of the Queen's Gambit Declined requires a not inconsiderable amount of theoretical knowledge.

7 ♗xc4

Less common but interesting is 7 e5, a typical continuation being 7...cxd4 8 ♕a4+ ♘c6 9 0-0-0 ♗d7 10 ♘e4 ♗e7 11 exf6 gxf6 12 ♗h4 ♖c8 when Black has collected three pawns (and something to bite on) for a piece. The text is designed to keep White in the driving seat.

7...cxd4

With two pins on the board we won't be surprised to see Black's queen come to a5 soon, but the timing needs to be right. For example here 7...♕a5?! leads to a good game for White after 8 ♗xf6 ♗xc3+ 9 bxc3 ♕xc3+ 10 ♘d2 gxf6 11 dxc5 because Black has nothing to show for his damaged kingside pawns, whereas White is ready to castle.

8 ♘xd4 ♗xc3+

Again it is important to find – or learn – the most accurate order of moves, for in the event of 8...♕a5 White can avoid the transposition to the game that follows 9 ♗xf6 ♗xc3+ 10 bxc3 ♕xc3+ in favour of 9 ♗d2! with a slight but definite pull.

9 bxc3 ♕a5 10 ♗b5+

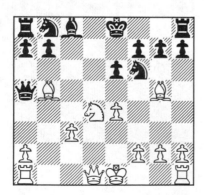

A key check. Despite what soon happens to his own king, White's strategy revolves around the permanent weaknesses in front of Black's king, and the text exploits a little tactic to create development problems for the defender. This, in turn, will earn White added time later when his attack gets under way.

10...♘bd7

Black would prefer not to be tied up but 10...♗d7 11 ♗xf6 works out well for White. The first point to note is that 11...♕xc3+? 12 ♔f1 gxf6 runs into 13 ♖c1

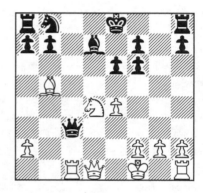

For some reason pins on bishops by bishops can cause confusion, and here ♖c8+ will follow the queen's retreat. Forced, therefore, is 11...gxf6, when 12 ♕b3 guarantees White an advantage, e.g. 12...0-0 13 0-0 ♘c6 (after 13...♗xb5 14 ♘xb5 ♘c6 15 c4 Black's kingside damage is more significant than the isolated c-pawn) 14 ♗xc6 ♗xc6 15 ♘xc6 bxc6 16 ♖ae1, as in Khenkin-Rechlis, Tel Aviv 1992, or 12...a6 13 ♗e2 ♘c6 14 0-0 0-0 15 ♖ad1, Eingorn-Gelfand, Debrecen 1989.

11 ♗xf6 ♕xc3+

By now it is too late to change the

strategy as 11...gxf6 12 0-0 gives White too much harmony.

12 ♔f1

This minor inconvenience is what slows White down enough for Black to be able to accept the gambit pawn.

12...gxf6 13 h4

Bringing the rook into the game with h2-h4 and ♖h3 is a habit we all grow out of once we appreciate the wonders of castling, but here the circumstances dictate that White mobilise his forces before Black can unravel. Moreover, the rook will enter the arena with tempo. Notice that Black's modest material lead seems barely noticeable when we consider his development problems. In fact it is the pin that Black now addresses.

13...a6

13...♔e7 also escapes the pin but attacks nothing, affording White more time so that after 14 ♖h3 ♕a5 15 ♖b1 the development advantage grows further (15...♖d8 16 ♕c1!).

14 ♖h3 ♕a5 15 ♗e2 ♘c5?!

The '?!' is Kramnik's own, although finding good, safe moves here is difficult even for a strong GM such as Kaidanov. And herein lies the traditional problem in accepting (decent) long-term

gambits – when the sortie is over and the material collected, the 'keeping the head above water' phase of the defender's task requires both good moves and good nerves. This is particularly relevant when the queen has been used to pick up the pawn(s), perhaps the most common gambit scenario.

Tucking the king on e7 is an alternative, when 15...♔e7 16 ♖c1 ♖d8 17 ♕c2 ♘e5 18 ♕b2 ♖d6 19 ♖b3 has been assessed as clearly better for White, P.Cramling-Rodriguez Talavera, Dos Hermanas 1992 continuing 19...b5 20 f4 ♘c4 21 ♗xc4 bxc4 22 ♖xc4 ♗d7 23 a4 ♖d8 24 e5

White had managed to maintain her lead. Note in these variations that White's own king position is not a worry. 15...♕e5 is another option, while White's compensation is evident after 15...0-0 16 ♖g3+ ♔h8 17 ♕c1 ♖g8 18 ♖xg8+ ♔xg8 19 ♕h6.

16 ♘b3!

All of White's pieces have easy access to the game whereas Black is relying on the queen and knight to fight the battle, so Kramnik does not miss the opportunity to eliminate half the enemy's active force, leaving the queen to do all the work again.

16...♘xb3 17 ♕xb3 e5

Black hopes to give the bishop a decent outpost on e6 in order to try and bolster the defences. 17...♕e5 is mentioned in *NCO*, while Akopian-C.Horvath, Niksic 1991 went 17...♕c7 18 ♖d1 ♗d7

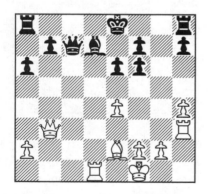

Black's extra pawn is still intact and he has managed to nudge his bishop forward, but White has made more progress and his major pieces threaten to band together and invade. There followed 19 ♕b2!, when Black was finally able to send his king to 'safety' with 19...0-0-0, although with 20 ♖c1 ♗c6 21 ♗xa6! ♖d6 (21...bxa6 22 ♖xc6 ♕xc6 23 ♖c3 favours White's queen and su-

perior pawns) 22 ♗e2 ♖hd8!? 23 ♕xf6 ♖d2 24 ♖a3 White succeeded in converting the initiative and the lead in development to a safe extra pawn.

18 ♖f3

Putting the rook on the g-file is also possible. Instead the f6-pawn is to be the focus of White's attention. Remember that White is not worried about regaining the gambit pawn. It was not sacrificed to merely be won back a few moves later, rather to gain time and exploit Black's resulting tardy development. The fact that the text hits the f6-pawn is relevant only in terms of how Black's defensive task would be accentuated if it falls – both e5 and f7 will be weaker without the f6-pawn.

18...♕d8

After 18...♔e7 19 ♖c1 followed by ♖fc3 the threatened infiltration on the seventh rank will have more impact with the king standing on e7. According to *NCO* White has an edge after the consistent 18...♗e6 19 ♕xb7 0-0 20 ♕e7 ♕d8

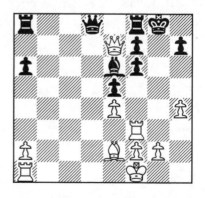

Indeed 21 ♕xf6 (21 ♕c5!? is a suggestion of Kramnik) 21...♕xf6 22 ♖xf6 ♖fd8 23 ♖f3 ♖d2 24 a3 (24...♗g4? 25 ♖g3) looks like an uphill struggle for

Black, although this might be preferable to the game continuation.

19 ♖c1!

19 ♖d1?! ♕e7 helps Black. White needs to look at the c7-square for a way in. The gambit pawn is becoming increasingly irrelevant with each improvement of White's powerful pieces.

19...♕e7?!

Perhaps not best. Nor is 19...♗g4?! 20 ♖d3 ♗xe2+ 21 ♔xe2 ♕e7 22 ♕b6, e.g. 22...♖d8 23 ♖c7, or 22...♕e6 23 ♕xe6+ fxe6 24 ♖c7 etc. 19...b5 keeps White's queen out of b6 but abandons c6, and Black is clearly worse after 20 ♖c6 ♗e6 21 ♕a3! ♕e7 22 ♗xb5! ♕xa3 23 ♖xa6+ ♔e7 24 ♖fxa3.

19...0-0 needs investigating: 20 ♕e3 ♔h8 21 ♕h6 and Black must be careful, e.g. 21...♗e6 22 ♖d3 ♕e7 23 ♖c7! (Kramnik), or 21...♖g8 22 ♖d3 ♕e7 23 ♖c7! ♕e6 24 ♖d6!

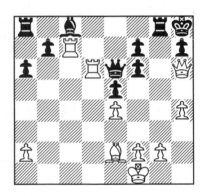

24...♕xd6 25 ♖xf7 ♗f5 26 exf5 etc.

Forced is 22...♕f8 23 ♕xf6+ ♕g7, when White is doing rather well.

20 ♕b6 ♕d8

A good illustration of the long-term nature of White's gambit strategy is 20...0-0 21 ♖c7 ♕e6 (21...♕d8 22 ♖d3) 22 ♖xf6 ♕xb6 23 ♖xb6

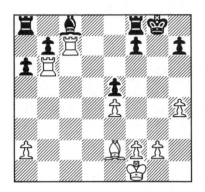

Just as the exchange of knights helped White (or did not help Black), so the trade of queens has failed to diminish White's pull. White has even regained the pawn.

20...♕e6!? 21 ♖xf6 ♕xb6 22 ♖xb6 ♗e6 is an attempt to break out that might offer Black the best chances.

21 ♖c7 ♕d4 22 ♖e7+!

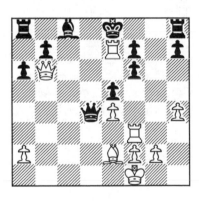

The beginning of the end.

22...♔xe7

There is no escape: 22...♔f8 23 ♖xf7+ ♔g8 24 ♖g7+! ♔xg7 25 ♕xf6+ etc.

23 ♕xf6+ ♔d7 24 ♖d3

And absolutely NOT 24 ♕xh8?? ♕a1+.

24...♕xd3 25 ♗xd3 ♖e8

25...♖f8 26 ♗c4.

26 ♗c4 ♖e7 27 ♗xf7

Black's development problem is a major factor even now.

27...♔d8

Unfortunately Black has no time for 27...b5 in view of 28 ♗d5 ♖a7 29 ♗c6+ ♔d8 30 ♕f8+.

28 ♕b6+ ♔d7

28...♖c7 29 ♗h5.

29 ♗b3 ♔e8 30 ♗a4+ ♔f7

Or 30...♗d7 31 ♗xd7+ ♖xd7 32 ♕e6+ ♔d8 33 ♕g8+.

31 ♕d8 1-0

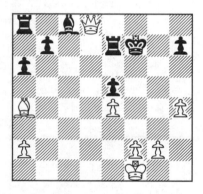

White's last highlights the fact that, after thirty moves, two of Black's pieces remain seated.

Unzicker-Patzl
Krems 1967

1 e4 e5 2 ♘f3 ♘c6 3 ♗b5 ♘d4 4 ♘xd4 exd4 5 d3 ♗b4+

The wrong plan. If Black wants to trade off his d4-pawn he shouldn't play the Bird's Variation. After 5...♗c5 6 0-0 c6 7 ♗a4 d6 8 ♗b3 ♘e7 9 f4 White has an edge.

6 c3 dxc3 7 ♘xc3! ♕f6 8 0-0 ♗xc3 9 bxc3

We reach decision time for Black, although it seems from his play thus far that he has already set his course. Already behind in development, best now is the sensible 9...♘e7 followed by castling, ...d7-d6 etc. But White's pawn is on offer.

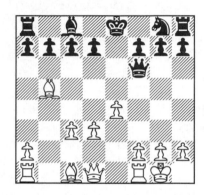

9...♕xc3?

The '?' is based on practical considerations. Elsewhere '??' has been used, but that is unfair because accepting the gambit is by no means a terrible blunder. However, Black is not in a position to enjoy the luxury of multiple queen moves.

10 ♖b1 ♕f6

White threatened ♗b2 and ♗xg7, and the text is preferable to 10...♘f6 11 ♕f3!, adding weight to ♗b2 and monitoring d5 in preparation for e4-e5. A feasible continuation is 11...♕c5 12 e5 ♘d5 13 d4 ♕e7 14 ♗c4! (14 ♕xd5 c6) and Black's king will be caught in the centre after either 14...♘b6 15 ♗a3 d6 16 ♗b5+ or 14...c6 15 ♗xd5 cxd5 16 ♗a3

See following diagram

Just as naturally good moves tend to play themselves, one poor idea or mistake often follows another. Here the price to pay for first surrendering a bishop for a knight and then sending the queen around the board for the reward of a single pawn is a stranded king. Even worse is 12...♕xe5 13 ♗a3 etc.

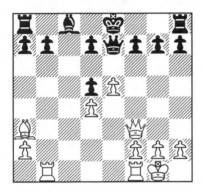

11 ♗b2 ♕g6

In the event of 11...♕h6 White can gain more time at the expense of Black's queen even by offering a trade: 12 ♕c1! ♕xc1 13 ♖fxc1 and both c7 and g7 are under fire.

12 f4!?

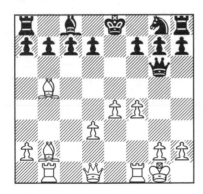

Preparing to hit the queen again.

12...♘f6

12...♕b6+ 13 ♔h1 ♕xb5 14 ♗xg7 is out of the question, and 12...f6 addresses the problem on one diagonal

while walking into difficulties on another, e.g. 13 ♕c2 c6 14 ♗c4.

13 f5 ♕h6

Black, who has moved his queen five times, is ready to castle. 13...♕h5 14 ♖f3! 0-0? 15 ♗xf6 gxf6 16 ♖g3+ is one to avoid.

14 ♗a3!

Obvious and best.

14...a6 15 ♗c4 b5

Unfortunately for Black, 15...d6 meets with a further investment: 16 e5! dxe5 17 ♕e2 ♘d7 18 d4 and the pressure mounts.

16 e5!?

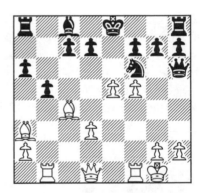

With such a lead in development any complications favour the attacker. Black is simply ill-prepared to cope with the inevitable opening of the position.

16...♕e3+

Black has no time to regroup after 16...bxc4 17 exf6 ♕xf6 18 ♖e1+ ♔d8 19 ♗e7+ ♕xe7 20 ♖xe7 ♔xe7 as 21 ♕e2+ is too fast, e.g. 21...♔d8 22 f6! (22...gxf6 23 ♕f3).

17 ♔h1 ♘e4

17...♘g8 18 ♗xf7+ ♔xf7 19 ♕h5+ g6 20 fxg6+.

18 ♗xf7+

More brutal than 18 dxe4 bxc4 19

♕d5.

18...♔d8

18...♔xf7 19 ♕h5+.

19 ♗c1!

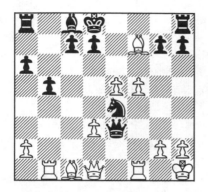

The final embarrassment.

19...♘f2+ 20 ♖xf2 ♕xf2 21 ♗g5
mate.

Schulten-Morphy
First American Chess Congress 1857

1 e4 e5 2 f4 d5 3 exd5 e4

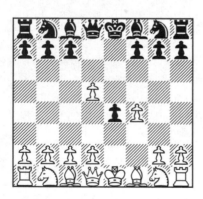

By declining the famous King's Gambit in this fashion Black seeks to make the f4-pawn look awkwardly placed. For example in some lines of this opening White's bishop is quite effective on f4 but in this case it will be hindered, and the open g1-a7 and e1-h4 lines might prove problematic for White. However, we can note that Black is yet to move a piece, and one of his centre pawns has already gone, so with accurate play White should gain an edge by striking quickly in the centre.

4 ♘c3

Right idea, wrong execution. Clearly the presence of the e4-pawn must be addressed, and this hits the pawn while developing a piece, so best is 4 d3 ♘f6 5 dxe4 ♘xe4 6 ♘f3, when White threatens to quickly castle and eventually emerge with the extra pawn safely intact, e.g. 6...♗c5 7 ♕e2 ♕xd5 8 ♘fd2 ♗f2+ 9 ♔d1 f5 10 ♘c3, or 7...♗f5 8 ♘c3 ♕e7 9 ♗e3 ♗xe3 10 ♕xe3 ♘xc3 11 ♕xe7+ ♔xe7 12 bxc3 ♗xc2 13 ♔d2 and the return of the pawn has given White a useful lead in development.

4...♘f6 5 d3 ♗b4 6 ♗d2 e3!?

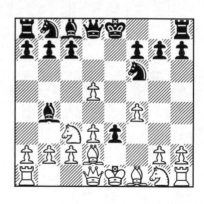

Black offers his second centre pawn, this time to speed up development soon by exploiting the open e-file and the renewed pin on the knight. Notice that from this point on the role of the f4-pawn is as the (conspicuous) villain of the piece, being the cause of events behind it yet powerless to influence them.

7 ♗xe3 0-0

There is nothing stopping Black from picking up the d5-pawn here or on the next move, reducing the gambit tally to just one pawn while maintaining a pull. However, Morphy, like Tal a century or so later, never worried about the 'score' – rather he let his deep appreciation of dynamics help him steer the game to the complex situations in which he excelled (and in which his opponents would struggle). The text threatens to pin the bishop, which could prove awkward, hence White's next.

8 ♗d2

8 h3?! was seen in Afinogenova-Yurtaev, Kstovo 1994. This is a poor move indeed, keeping both knight and bishop out of g4 but at the cost of a tempo White can ill afford here. But it is White's calm, deliberate and foolhardy use of her king in this game that I thought deserved attention, as this is, in fact, not such an unusual reaction when faced with gambit play. There followed 8...♘xd5 9 ♔f2 ♘xe3 10 ♔xe3 ♘c6 11 ♘f3 ♖e8+ 12 ♔f2 ♘d4 13 ♔g3 ♖e3 14 ♕d2 ♕d6!?

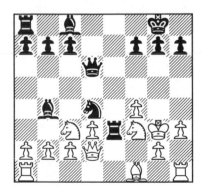

15 ♖e1 (15 ♕xe3? ♘f5+) 15...♗c5 16 ♔f2 (16 ♖xe3 still runs into 16...♘f5+)

16...♘xf3 and White resigned in view of 17 gxf3 ♖xd3+. We learn from the games in this book that spending time to pick up gambit pawns with the queen is indeed quite risky, but sending the king out to battle in gambit situations is, to put it mildly, foolhardy.

Black cuts across his opponent's plans after 8 ♘f3 ♖e8, e.g. 9 ♘e5 ♘xd5, when c3, e3 and e5 (after ...f7-f6 in the event of 10 ♗d2) cannot be adequately covered.

8...♗xc3

The immediate 8...♖e8+ offers White another option. A good illustration of greedy play leading to poor, compromised piece placement is the position after 9 ♘ce2 ♗c5 10 c4 ♘g4 11 ♘h3.

White's latest 'development' defends f2, one of two squares under fire on the g1–a7 diagonal. Black now turns his attention to the other diagonal left open by the f-pawn. 11...♕h4+ 12 g3 ♘xh2!

A dream position for the gambiteer, following up the pawns with an offer of his queen – an offer, of course, that can indeed be refused in view of the visual mate on f3. However, White's days are numbered. Detko-Bedac, Slovakia 1998 ended 13 ♕c2 ♕xg3+ 14 ♔d1 ♕f3 0-1, while Sonnenberger-Zickelbein, Bundesliga 1994 should have seen another queen offer after 13 ♕a4 ♘f3+ (13...♖xe2+ 14 ♗xe2 ♕xg3+ 15 ♔d1 ♗xh3 looks good, e.g. 16 ♕e8+ ♗f8 17 ♗b4 ♘c6 18 ♕xa8 ♘xb4 etc.) 14 ♔d1 ♕e7 15 ♗c3 ♕e3 16 ♔c2 ♗d7 17 ♕a5, when Black has 17...♕xd3+!

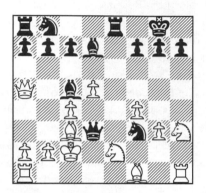

A forced mate will follow. If only gambits led so smoothly to such a nice finish. Obviously this is not the case, but at least the advantages that accompany successful gambit play are more likely to create circumstances in which such possibilities exist, and where mistakes are more common.

9 bxc3 ♖e8+ 10 ♗e2 ♗g4

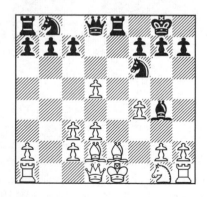

11 c4?

Not best. The four centre pawns might look good but the attraction ends there. 11 h3 transposes to Vyskocil-Blaha, Czech Team Championship 1996. Black ignored the threat and replied 11...♕xd5, when after 12 ♔f2 the simple 12...♗xe2 13 ♘xe2 ♕c5+ 14 ♔g3 ♘c6 would have offered some compensation, albeit not a pawn's worth.

Another game went 11 ♔f2 ♗xe2 12 ♘xe2 ♕xd5 13 ♖e1 ♘c6 14 ♔g1 ♕c5+ 15 d4 ♕f5, when White had managed to castle 'by hand' but the holes on c4 and e4 provided Black's knights with good squares (d5 is another one), a draw eventually resulting in Castellanos-Arribas, Ciego de Avila 1997.

11...c6!

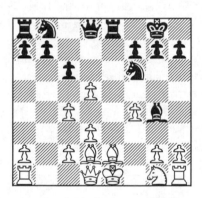

The d5-pawn is challenged anyway, presenting White with a problem – allow ...c6xd5, when the situation is repeated with the c4-pawn, or accelerate Black's development. White opts for the latter scenario.

12 dxc6 ♘xc6

Now another piece threatens to hit e2.

13 ♔f1

13 ♗c3 ♘d4 14 ♗xd4 ♕xd4 sees an

even more dangerous piece come to d4, and White's development problems accentuated. The two extra pawns mean absolutely nothing, e.g. 15 ♖b1 ♖xe2+ 16 ♘xe2 ♖e8 etc.

13...♖xe2!

Setting up a second, more deadly pin.

14 ♘xe2 ♘d4

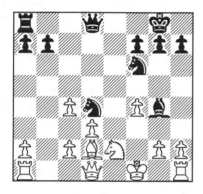

Life is getting even more uncomfortable for White who, by now, must have been regretting his material over development policy.

15 ♕b1 ♗xe2+

With White's rooks still in the corners, contributing nothing to the game, the minor pieces will decide. The game continued:

16 ♔f2 ♘g4+ 17 ♔g1

Fritz announces 'mate in 7' here. Morphy delivers.

17...♘f3+! 18 gxf3 ♕d4+ 19 ♔g2 ♕f2+ 20 ♔h3 ♕xf3+ 21 ♔h4 ♘e3 22 ♖g1 ♘f5+ 23 ♔g5 ♕h5 mate

A poor display from White, but nonetheless typical at club level.

There is a rule that in open positions a pawn equates to three tempi. This is a rough guide, of course, and it is assumed that the sacrifice is decent, but the examples in this book demonstrate that three tempi can be too much to give away. It is important not to restrict this way of thinking just to open positions, although these do offer more scope for such gambits. Once we have these possibilities in mind we can look for ways of offering a pawn or pawns for tempi which themselves can lead to a favourable opening of the position, and this is best combined with a development advantage. The sooner we approach the game with this versatile, relaxed – even optimistic – attitude the better, particularly for juniors. Being afraid to part with pawns is a habit that can be difficult to shake off.

In the following game White, aged thirteen, demolishes his opponent's French Defence by offering the centre pawns and bouncing off the enemy queen.

Trunov-Bessonov

Moscow Pioneers Palace 1982

1 e4 e6 2 d4 d5 3 e5

The French Defence is a difficult nut to crack, and the choice of White's system is down to taste and style. The Advance Variation is designed at containing Black and exploiting the space advantage on the kingside created by the pawn chain in the centre.

3...c5 4 c3 ♕b6 5 ♘f3 ♘c6 6 ♗d3

A tricky move depriving the d-pawn of a defender pawn, but setting up a nasty. If Black is to castle kingside then the b1-h7 diagonal would be perfect for the bishop, but the text is gambit-based. Consequently 6 ♗e2 and 6 a3 tend to be seen more often at higher levels.

6...♗d7

The trap into which inexperienced and very greedy, impulsive players might fall comes about after 6...cxd4 7 cxd4 ♘xd4? (7...♗d7 8 0-0 transposes to the game and is the usual move order, thus ruling out 7 dxc5) 8 ♘xd4 ♕xd4?? 9 ♗b5+

Checks accompanied by discovered attacks can often be devastating. This particular one picks up the queen. Such possibilities can play a big, albeit unrealistic part in attracting players to this or that opening or variation, which is probably the case for the young hopeful Trunov. However, he does conduct the rest of the game in fine style, demonstrating that he undoubtedly possesses a healthy understanding of the importance of the concepts time and development.

7 0-0

I remember reading many years ago that 6...♗d7?! is an inaccuracy because it presents White with a reason to take on c5 with advantage, the point being that after 7 dxc5 ♗xc5 8 0-0 the natural 8...♘ge7? sees the bishop without a retreat in the case of 9 b4. Consequently Black's development is disrupted, usually with a tempo spent on ...a7-a5, addressing White's queenside expansion involving b2-b4. But White has played the move 6 ♗d3 with the intention of a gambit or two, and he sticks to the strategy.

7...cxd4 8 cxd4 ♘xd4 9 ♘xd4 ♕xd4

This time Black's queen survives because there is no check on b5. Of course there is more to this line than the chance to net a queen. Giving up a pawn in the hope of this happening is a pure gamble rather than a gambit, and an appreciation of this distinction is important.

By now we should be getting used to the idea of inviting in the enemy queen for a trade of pawns for tempi. Black might not have donated his queen by snatching the d4-pawn earlier, but in return for the pawn White can expect to exploit the exposed queen to gain at least a couple more developing moves which, considering his current lead and Black's tardy kingside, might prove interesting. A popular move here is 10 ♕e2, but it is also possible to continue in gambit style and ignore the threat to the e5-pawn, a policy well suited to the cavalier, initiative driven, aggressive style of a promising young Muscovite schoolboy.

10 ♘c3 ♕xe5

The battle of contrasting styles continues, with Black adding the second gambit pawn to the collection. However, isn't one pawn enough? Accepting a gambit pawn in itself can be a tricky proposition, but doubling the material gain often means at least doubling the inconvenience, which is why the 'happy medium' 10...a6 is a recommended recipe for Black here. This does, I admit, spend a tempo on a defensive nudge of a queenside pawn when the kingside forces are conspicuously still, but defending b5 is sensible and in fact makes development both safer and easier for Black. *NCO* gives 11 ♕e2 ♘e7 12 ♔h1 ♘c6 13 f4 ♘b4 14 ♖d1 ♗c5 15 ♗xa6 ♕f2 16 ♕xf2 ♗xf2 as an edge for Black.

11 ♖e1 ♕d6

The alternative 11...♕b8 12 ♘xd5 ♗d6 leads to an unclear position, Black returning one of the pawns in order to engineer some kind of activity. Instead the two pawn lead remains intact, but this in turn is directly related to White's

development lead, which therefore continues to grow.

12 ♕f3

White keeps up the momentum and prepares to bring out another piece at the expense of Black's queen. Another (perhaps preferable) option is 12 ♘b5, when Djurhuus-Shulman, Gausdal 1994 went 12...♗xb5 13 ♗xb5+ ♔d8 14 ♕h5 ♕e7 15 ♗f4 ♘f6 16 ♕e5

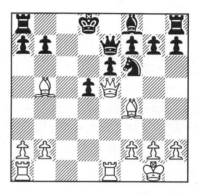

It is interesting to see how two strong players cope with their respective roles in this gambit situation. Fortunately for Black the extra pawns provide a defensive wall against White's major pieces, although the bishops work well with the queen. Having the king on d8 is the biggest worry, leaving White in no hurry because Black's lack of co-ordination and general problems are here to stay. The game continued 16...♕c5 17 a4 a6 18 ♗d3 ♘d7 19 ♗g5+ ♔e8 20 ♕e2 ♗e7 21 ♗f4 ♗d6 22 ♗d2 ♘e5 23 ♖ac1 ♕d4 24 ♗b1 and another pawn was on the menu. With ♗c3 coming, Black accepted: 24...♕xb2 25 ♖c2 ♕b6 26 ♗a2 ♔d7 27 ♖b1 (exploiting another opened file) 27...♕a7 28 ♗f4 ♘c6 29 ♗e3 d4 30 ♕f3 f5 31 ♗f4 ♗xf4 32 ♕xf4 g6 33 ♗xe6+

Something like this had to happen eventually, otherwise Black would consolidate. Whether the crucial break-through sacrifice is sound is another matter but, in practical terms, it is consistent and quite necessary. Black might even believe it himself and search for a route to safety that is unfavourable but at least puts an end to the pressure (a common defensive 'resource' when a better but complex, nerve-jangling option is available). There followed 33...♔xe6 34 ♕c7 ♕b8 (34...♖ab8 loses to 35 ♖xc6+, but the odd 34...♖hb8 is possible, inviting a bizarre bind after 35 ♖b6) 35 ♖e1+ ♔f6 36 ♖xc6+ ♔g5 (36...bxc6 37 ♕e7 mate) 37 ♕e7+ ♔h5

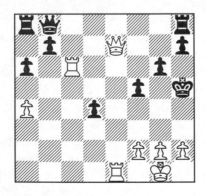

After the investments were returned

in instalments White eventually converted a queen ending, winning an epic battle on the 110th move. I don't believe White's compensation was enough in the initial diagram position, but this evaluation, crucially, is based on 'best play', and we all know what a tall order that is. As far as real life is concerned, Djurhuus was perfectly aware of the practical difficulties experienced by Black and the psychological implications of the development problems. Psychology plays a major part in gambit play and should not be underestimated.

12...♗c6!

Black finally seeks refuge for his queen, simultaneously improving the bishop. Crepan-Kozamernik, Bled 1998, saw the queen go on another pawn grabbing mission: 12...♘e7 13 ♗f4 ♕b4 14 ♕g3 ♗c6 15 ♗d6 ♕xb2 16 ♘b5

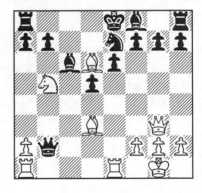

Now Black could consider 16...♘f5!, when the entertaining 17 ♗xf5 ♕xb5 18 ♗xf8 ♔xf8 19 ♕d6+ ♔g8 20 ♗xe6 ♖f8 21 ♖ad1 leaves Black tied up but White is running out of resources, although a draw would not be a surprise. Instead the game continued in the same fashion: 16...♗xb5 17 ♖ab1 ♕xa2 18 ♗xb5+ ♘c6 (18...♔d8 19 ♗c7+ ♔c8 20

♗d8!) 19 ♗xf8 ♔xf8 20 ♗xc6 bxc6 21 ♕d6+ ♔e8 22 ♖b7 and White won.

Here 19...♖xf8 leads to a draw after 20 ♗xc6+ bxc6 21 ♖b8+ ♖xb8 22 ♕xb8+ ♔e7 23 ♕c7+ ♔f6 24 ♕f4+ and so on, but 21 ♕d6 again seems strong, e.g. 21...♕a6 22 ♖xe6+ fxe6 23 ♕xe6+ ♔d8 24 ♕d6+, or 21...♕d2 22 ♕xc6+ ♔e7 23 ♖b7+ ♔f6 24 ♖xf7+!

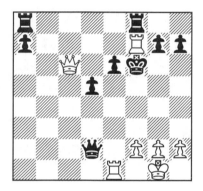

While we like to reassure ourselves that there is no need to worry about being a pawn or two down – or in this case, three – when in gambit mode, we are only human, and this is easier said than done. It is when an initiative seems to have come to an end, compensation has dried up or when the opposition has defended well (or we have followed up a gambit inadequately) that some inspiration is called for, and this decisive rook sacrifice is a good example of the gambiteer's optimism bringing results. I have been fortunate enough to edit a few of Danish IM Jacob Aagaard's excellent books, and one piece of many snippets of invaluable advice he gives is to think of what you would like to play and then see if you can make it happen, however unlikely it might appear at first sight. Here the f7-pawn provides the crucial e6-square with protection.

13 ♗f4 ♕d7 14 ♗e5

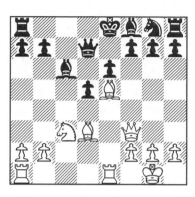

Remember that White was only thirteen when this game was played, so the text is impressive in view of its aim to hinder Black's already awkward development. Consequently Black is left once again to weigh up the pros and cons of how to address this latest challenge.

14...f6 15 ♗d4

Threatening ♗f5 etc.

15...e5?!

15...♗e7 16 ♕g4 ♔f7 might not look too nice for Black but 17 ♕h5+ ♔f8 18 ♗xh7 is a self-pin, so White should perhaps look for other ways to maintain the pressure.

16 ♗f5 ♕f7 17 ♕h3

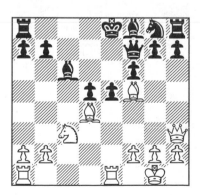

Followed by ♗e6 with another attack on the queen.

17...♗d7

Again Black reacts to the threat, challenging White's control of the diagonal and forcing a trade of bishops, a policy of exchanges that is recommended as a means to relieve pressure in these difficult defensive situations. However, sometimes this means removing from the arena – or from a key post – a useful defensive piece.

Allowing the infiltration with 17...♘e7 leads to an interesting position after 18 ♗e6 ♕g6 19 ♖ad1, when White's forces are primed for action, and Black is in yet another situation that requires a decision – find a constructive move that does not give White a free hand, or call White's bluff and accept the conversion of the two pawn lead into a whole piece after 19...exd4 20 ♘xd5 ♗xd5 21 ♗xd5 ♖d8 22 ♖xd4

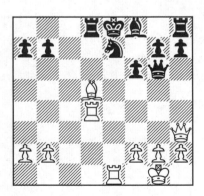

Black does have an extra piece, but he is seriously tied up.

Returning to the position after 17...♗d7, it is time for White to strike while the iron is hot and take full advantage of his larger, menacing army.

18 ♗xe5!

It would be illogical and inconsistent to slow down at this stage of the game, particularly when Black's centre is at its most vulnerable.

18...♗xf5

Not 18...fxe5 19 ♖xe5+ ♔d8 20 ♗xd7 (20...♕xd7 21 ♖xd5).

19 ♗f4+ ♗e4 20 ♘b5 ♖d8 21 ♘c7+ ♔e7 22 ♕a3+

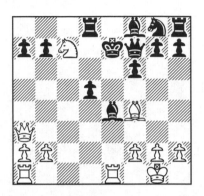

Did you see this one?

22...♔d7 23 ♕a4+ ♔e7

23...b5 24 ♕xa7 looks decisive, while 23...♔c8 24 ♖ac1 is even quicker.

24 ♕b4+?!

24 ♖xe4+! wraps up as 24...dxe4 25 ♕xe4+ ♔d7 26 ♕f5+ forces mate.

24...♔d7 25 ♕xb7

25 ♕a4+ is also fine.

25...♗d6

Black cannot survive, e.g. 25...f5 26 ♖ad1.

26 ♗xd6 ♔xd6 27 ♘b5+

An instructive display in practical gambit play, and full marks for effort.

Spassky-Osnos
31st USSR Ch, Leningrad 1963

1 d4 ♘f6 2 ♘f3 e6 3 ♗g5

Because White can employ the Torre

Attack against ...d7-d5, ...g7-g6 and ...e7-e6 systems it is, not surprisingly, a fairly popular choice, particularly at club level.

3...c5

This immediate strike in the centre is designed – in conjunction with a quick ...♛b6 – to exploit the early development of White's bishop by hitting the now slightly-weakened b2-square. Some Torre players who are not used to parting with a pawn or two hope not to face this reply, while others relish the opportunity to race into a menacing development lead at the expense of Black's queen.

4 e3

The most popular, promising move. Also possible is 4 c3, anticipating 4...♛b6 but running the 'risk' of allowing a symmetrical structure along the lines of the solid Exchange Slav after 4...cxd4 5 cxd4 etc. However, unsuspecting players intent on grabbing the b-pawn can be in for a nasty surprise (4 c3 ♛b6): 5 ♞bd2 ♛xb2 6 ♞c4 ♛xc3+? (the better alternative 6...♛b5 7 e4 ♛c6 8 ♝d3 is sufficiently complicated to justify doing some homework) 7 ♝d2 ♛xc4 8 e4

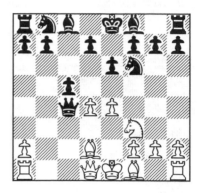

Not a simple means of trapping a queen and, consequently, a predicament into which Black can be forgiven for finding himself. A couple of pieces and pawns can be recouped but White will stand much better.

4...♛b6 5 ♞bd2

The unambitious 5 ♛c1 leads only to equality after 5...♞e4 6 ♝f4 d5 etc. Of course this does not rule out what might be an interesting, heavyweight manoeuvring battle of wits, and White need not worry about being material down. But on the other hand, for example, Black is not put under any pressure, suffers no structural damage and does not lag behind in development after 5 ♛c1. There is also the psychological aspect to consider. With ...♛b6 Black is already putting out a feeler as to his opponent's psyche – a useful tool at this stage of the game. Not only is Black doing fine when White defends b2, he has also discovered – at no cost – that White is probably uncomfortable in, or even unwilling to enter, certain types of position or situation, and this knowledge can be exploited as the game progresses. Being happy to gambit the b-pawn (and any subsequent pawns) sends a signal to Black that this version of the Torre Attack is indeed your territory.

5...♛xb2

With so few moves being played thus far it is not possible to measure White's compensation, suffice to say that the final minor piece is ready to enter the game, Black's exposed queen is sure to provide White with further gain of time and a trade on f6 (should White be prepared to let the Torre bishop go) will break up Black's pawns. These factors in themselves should be enough to justify the gambit.

6 ♗d3

Simply bringing out another piece, this is the most flexible option. When in doubt as to formulating a plan in the opening phase it makes sense to improve. A major alternative is to add structure to time with 6 ♗xf6 gxf6. Then 7 ♖b1 ♛xa2 8 ♘c4 ♛a4 9 d5 b5 10 ♘cd2 a6 11 ♖a1 ♛b4 12 c4 ♗b7 13 e4 offered some compensation in a complex position in Ye Rongguang-Chandler, Manila Interzonal 1990. More popular is 7 ♗d3 ♛c3 8 0-0 d5 with a further branch.

J.Benjamin-Yudasin, New York Open 1990 provided a good illustration of how to cope with this kind of situation from Black's side of the board. Remember that White has surrendered his dark-squared bishop to create doubled f-pawns, and that the exchange has given Black a half-open g-file to work with (not an unattractive proposition given that White has already castled short). Consequently it is not illogical for Black to seek to generate play based on these factors. This particular game continued 9 dxc5!? ♗g7 10 ♖b1 ♛xc5 11 e4 dxe4 12 ♘xe4 ♛c7, and now after 13 ♗b5+ Black decided not to block the check and instead volunteered 13...♔f8, when an unclear situation arose after the active defence 14 ♛d2 a6 15 ♗e2 ♘c6 16 ♖fd1 h5! 17 ♘d6 h4 18 ♖b3 h3 19 g3 ♖h5!? 20 ♖d3 ♛a5

Black is still behind in development and White enjoys more control of the centre, but at least the g7-bishop has potential (and will face no genuine challenge should it begin to make an impact on the game), the h3-pawn gives White something to think about on the back rank and Black's queen and rook have got a partnership going, albeit a rather unconventional one. This is how Black should play, but I get the feeling that it is not to everyone's taste, that most players wouldn't recognise the push of the h-pawn as a thematic plan and, even if they did, would lack the confidence to execute it.

It is when ostensibly unorthodox play is among the more successful strategies of dealing with certain lines that the gambit is all the more promising. If confidence, versatility and a not inconsiderable helping of talent are important characteristics for the defender we should be willing to invest more time getting acquainted with such a gambit oriented system.

Raetsky-Pripis, USSR 1988 saw 9 ♗b5+ ♗d7 10 ♖b1 cxd4 11 ♘xd4 ♘c6 12 ♖b3 ♕a5 13 c4 ♖d8 14 ♕e2 a6 15 cxd5 axb5 16 dxc6 bxc6 17 ♘e4 ♗e7 18 ♖c1 f5 19 ♘c5 ♗xc5 20 ♖xc5 ♖a8 21 a3

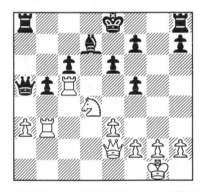

White has converted his development advantage into a structural one, although Black is still trailing. White owns the dark squares and has the classic good knight versus bad bishop ending to look forward to. And his king is safer. In fact Black sought to improve his lot by returning the pawn, but after 21...♖a6 22 ♖bc3 ♕a4 23 h3! (these quiet, sensible moves can be very satis-

fying to play) 23...0-0 24 ♕h5 f6 25 ♕f3 e5 26 ♘xf5 ♗xf5 27 ♕xf5 ♕d1+ 28 ♔h2 ♕d6 29 ♕e4 White was on his way to a winning major piece ending of some sort, converting the full point on the 44th move.

6...cxd4

With 6...♕c3 7 0-0 d5 Black obstructs White's c-pawn while keeping the options open for his own, 8 ♖e1 giving Black a choice as to how to deal with the centre. In Alexeev-Balashov, USSR 1972 Black advanced with 8...c4, preventing a complete opening of the position and limiting White to just the e-file: 9 ♗f1 ♘c6 10 ♗xf6 gxf6 11 e4 ♔d8 12 ♖b1 ♗h6 13 exd5 exd5 14 ♖b5 and White was doing well (apart from ♖xd5+ White toys with ♘b1, which would force ...♕a1).

8...cxd4 led to a level game in Salov-Psakhis, Irkutsk 1986 after 9 ♘xd4 a6 10 ♘4f3 ♘c6 11 e4 ♗e7 12 exd5 ♘xd5 13 ♘e4 ♕a3 14 c4 ♘c3 15 ♕d2 ♘xe4 16 ♗xe4 f6 17 ♗f4 e5 18 ♖ad1 ♗g4! 19 ♖e3 ♕c5 20 ♗g3 0-0 21 ♕c2 f5 22 ♗d5+ ♔h8 23 ♗xc6 ♕xc6 24 ♗xe5 ♗f6 25 ♗xf6 ♕xf6 26 ♖de1 f4 27 ♖b3 etc. However, worth looking at is 9 ♗xf6! gxf6 10 e4!?

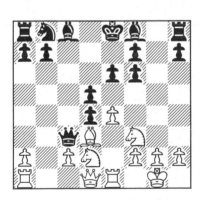

This idea was first tried in international practice in the game N.Ristic-Psakhis, Groningen 1995. Already way ahead in development, White can afford to ignore the d4-pawn and instead challenge its partner on d5. In this way he will succeed in opening up the game at a time when Black's only piece in play is the queen. In fact Psakhis fared less well this time around: 10...♕a5 11 ♘b3 ♕d8 (now Black has NO pieces developed and compromised pawns) 12 exd5 ♕xd5 13 ♘fxd4 ♘d7 14 c4 ♕g5 15 ♘b5 ♔d8 16 g3!? a6 (16...f5!?) 17 f4 ♕h6 18 ♘5d4

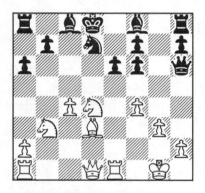

The tension mounts in White's favour. For example 18...♔c7 19 c5! ♘xc5 20 ♖c1 b6 21 ♗e4 ♗b7 22 ♗xb7 ♔xb7 23 ♕f3+ ♔a7 24 ♘xc5 ♗xc5 25 ♖xc5! bxc5 26 ♖b1 is a plausible continuation that will soon end in mate, while 18...♗b4 runs into the even more brutal 19 ♖xe6!! fxe6 20 ♘xe6+ ♔e7 21 ♘c7 ♘b6 (21...♖a7 22 ♘d5+ ♔f7 23 ♘xb4 keeps the fire burning for White) 22 c5 f5 23 ♕e2+ ♔f7 (23...♔d8 24 ♘xa8 ♘xa8 25 ♕b2 ♖e8 26 ♕d4+ is decisive) 24 ♗c4+ ♘xc4 (24...♔g6 25 cxb6) 25 ♕xc4+ ♗e6 26 ♕xb4 ♖ab8 27 ♖e1 is very awkward for Black.

In the game 18...♖g8 19 ♕f3 ♘c5 20 ♖ad1 ♔c7 (20...♘xd3 21 ♖xd3 ♔c7 22 c5 ♗d7 23 c6!) 21 ♗f1! ♗d7 22 ♗g2 ♖b8 23 ♔h1 ♕g6 24 ♕e3! b6 (24...♘xb3!?) 25 ♕f3 left Black's queen and rook looking out of it on the g-file. Then 25...♕g4 26 ♘xc5 ♗xc5 (26...bxc5 27 ♘xe6+! fxe6 28 ♖xd7+ ♔xd7 29 ♕c6+ ♔d8 30 ♗f3!) 27 ♘xe6+ fxe6 28 ♖xd7+ ♔xd7 29 ♕c6+ ♔d8 30 ♗f3 ♕g6 31 ♖d1+ ♔e7 32 ♕c7+ ♔f8 33 ♕xb8+ ♔g7 seems like a lesser evil for Black. In fact the struggle was soon over: 25...♗d6 26 ♘c6 ♖gc8 (26...♖bc8 27 ♘xc5 ♗xc5 [27...bxc5 28 ♘e7] 28 ♘e7! is funny) 27 ♘xb8 ♖xb8 28 ♘xc5 bxc5 29 ♕a3 ♖b6 30 ♕a5 1-0. The difference in the plight of the kings was crucial here.

With 6...d5 Black invites a rapid strike in the centre with 7 ♗xf6 gxf6 8 c4

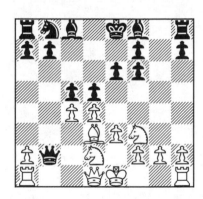

We see that as well as making finding a safe haven for Black's king more problematic, the trade on f6 of a potentially good bishop for a normal knight has also served to undermine Black's support of the centre. Now Pira-Verat, Paris 1990 was a demolition job: 8...♕c3 9 ♗e2 dxc4 10 0-0 ♘c6 11 ♘e4 ♕a5 12 d5 ♘b4 13 ♗xc4 b5 14 ♘xf6+

♔e7 15 ♘e5!? ♔xf6 16 ♕f3+ ♔e7 17 ♕xf7+ ♔d8 18 ♖fd1 1-0. Here 15...bxc4 16 ♕h5 spells the end, e.g. 16...♔xf6 17 f4 ♔e7 18 ♕xf7+ ♔d8 19 ♖ad1 etc.

Once again a more energetic remedy could be necessary. Witness Klinger-Granda Zuniga, Novi Sad Olympiad 1990: 8...b5!? 9 0-0 (9 ♖b1 ♕xa2 10 ♖xb5 might be better) 9...♕a3 10 ♕b1 bxc4 11 ♘xc4 ♕a6! 12 ♘ce5 c4 13 ♘xc4 dxc4 14 ♗e4 ♘c6 15 d5 ♖b8 16 ♕c2 ♘b4 17 ♕b2 exd5 18 ♗xd5 ♖b6 0-1.

Instead of 8 c4 White can also try 8 ♖b1 ♕c3 9 0-0, when Pira-Michalet, Paris 1990 saw another nice win for the amiable IM: 9...c4 10 ♗xc4 dxc4 11 ♘e4 ♕a5 12 ♘xf6+ ♔e7 13 ♘e5 ♘c6 14 ♕h5! ♘xe5 (14...♘d8 leaves the queen unprotected) 15 dxe5 ♗g7 16 ♖fd1 h6 17 ♖xb7+! 1-0

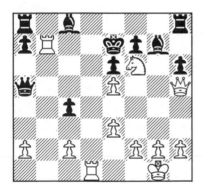

I'm sure I've seen at least one other game end in the same fashion. Certainly it is easy for Black to underestimate White's attack after the piece sacrifice on c4, which is why seeking to close the centre with gain of tempo on the bishop would make ...c5-c4 a plausible looking option.

Let us return to the position after 6...exd4:

7 exd4 ♕c3 8 0-0 d5 9 ♖e1

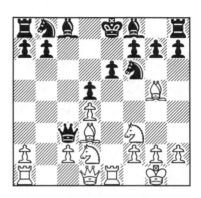

9...♗e7

Black finally supports the knight to rule out doubled pawns. After 9...♘c6 10 ♖b1 ♘xd4 11 ♘xd4 ♕xd4 12 ♘e4 the game hots up in White's favour (there's another nasty check after 12...dxe4 13 ♗b5+).

10 ♖e3

Threatening another check to pick up the queen, as well as activating the rook.

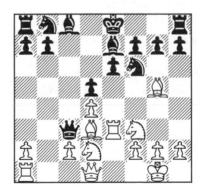

10...♕c7 11 ♘e5 ♘c6 12 c3 ♘xe5

With a fairly solid position Black might consider 12...♗d7 followed by ...♖c8. The text is rather committal, 'promoting' White's pawn to e5 and thereby hindering Black's development. Incidentally, 12...0-0 might be what Black has been waiting to play but walks into a classic sacrifice: 13 ♗xf6 ♗xf6 14 ♗xh7+!

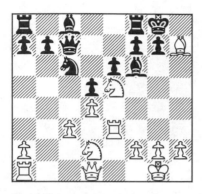

One to remember.

13 dxe5 ♘g8

13...♘d7 14 ♗xe7 ♔xe7 15 ♕g4 can't be what Black is looking for, e.g. 15...♘xe5 16 ♕xg7 or 15...♕xc3 16 ♕g5+ ♔e8 17 ♖d1 and Black is really struggling. With the text Black will be able to recapture on e7 with his knight, so White does not oblige.

14 ♘f3 h6?

Compounding Black's development problems. Again 14...♗d7 looks sensible, this time with the intention of castling long, although the king is not completely safe on the queenside, it has to be said.

15 ♗f4

Black's prospects have taken a downward turn over the last few moves, the trade on e5 severely restricting his breathing space and the knight now being locked in.

15...♗d7 16 ♘d4

White calmly improves his knight, sending it nearer the queenside in case

Black now decides to send his king there, which may well be the best course even if it does appear a little risky. Instead Black seeks to 'justify' ...h7-h6.

16...♗g5 17 ♗xg5 hxg5 18 ♕g4 ♕xc3

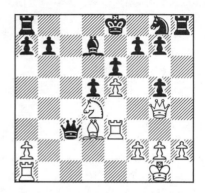

The queen returns to snaffle another pawn. As well as ...♕xa1 Black threatens ...♘h6 to kick the queen away from the defence of the knight on d4, but White is ready.

19 ♘b3! ♘h6 20 ♕xg5 ♕b4 21 ♖g3

Spassky prefers to turn the screw and prevent castling (in view of the mate on g7) rather than restore material equity with 21 ♕xg7, when 21...♕f8 22 ♕xf8+ should favour White's superior pieces.

21...♕f8

Apparently a 'distinguished British chess author' suggested 21...0-0-0 here! After 21...♕e7 White can consider 22 ♕e3, keeping an eye on the a7-pawn (and therefore preventing ...0-0-0) and planning to bring the second rook into play with ♖c1. This rook also plays a part in the event of 21...g6 22 ♖h3 ♕f8 23 ♖c1, when White fully exploits the switch to the c-file with 23...♖c8 24 ♖xc8+ ♗xc8 25 ♗b5+ ♗d7 26 ♖c3!

Note that 21...♖g8? runs into 22 ♕xh6! gxh6 23 ♖xg8+ ♔e7 24 ♖xa8, picking up two rooks and a knight for the queen.

22 ♖c1

Intending ♖c7 followed by ♘c5 etc. White is not interested in taking on g7 – such a possibility should not really feature on the agenda in consistent gambit play. It is more interesting to let Black keep guard over g7 and apply pressure in another sector.

22...f6

Again 22...♖c8 23 ♖xc8+ ♗xc8 24 ♗b5+ ♗d7 25 ♖c3 is decisive.

23 ♕e3 f5 24 ♘c5

White threatens both ♘xb7-d6+ and 25 ♘xd7, but 24...♗c6 drops the e6-pawn.

24...f4

Desperate, but 24...♗c8 is way too passive.

25 ♗g6+ ♔e7 26 ♕a3! 1-0

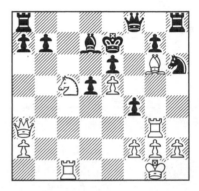

A possible finish is 26...♗c6 27 ♘xb7+ ♔d7 28 ♘c5+ ♔e7 29 ♘xe6+ etc.

This variation seems to offer White good practical chances, not least because a certain level of skill is required from Black if he is to prevent White's development advantage assuming decisive proportions.

CHAPTER TWO

Open Lines

This is a particularly easy concept to get to grips with. We know how well our pieces operate when given a little help in terms of their scope, so it is not beyond us to imagine giving up a pawn or two in order to quickly open lines for key pieces. Such gambits helped form the foundations upon which so-called coffee house chess was based in the good old days, but they also play a major part in modern practice.

Let us start with a classic from a previous era.

Anderssen-Dufresne
Berlin 1852

1 e4 e5 2 ♘f3 ♘c6 3 ♗c4 ♗c5 4 b4 ♗xb4 5 c3 ♗a5

see following diagram

In the heavyweight clash Kasparov-Anand (seen in Chapter 3) Black played the retreat 5...♗e7. The text instead keeps the bishop posted on the same diagonal as White's king, which is why the move 6 0-0 is an alternative to White's next.

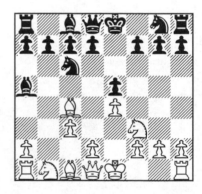

6 d4 exd4 7 0-0 d3

Black prefers to see this pawn leave the board on his terms rather than allow cxd4. 7...♘ge7 8 cxd4 d5 9 exd5 ♘xd5 10 ♗a3 ♗e6 sees Black block the e-file and prepare to obstruct the a3-bishop in order to castle. Then 11 ♗b5 f6 12 ♕a4 ♗b6 13 ♗xc6+ bxc6 14 ♕xc6+ ♔f7 returns the pawn but leaves Black a shade better thanks to the bishop pair. But 8 ♘g5 is interesting, e.g. 8...♘e5 9 ♘xf7 ♘xf7 10 ♗xf7+ ♔xf7 11 ♕h5+ g6 12 ♕xa5 with an edge to White, or 8...0-0? 9 ♕h5 h6 10 ♘xf7. Best is 8...d5 9 exd5 ♘e5 10 ♗b3 0-0, which was unclear in Bronstein-Al. Ivanov,

Maidstone 1994.

We should take a look at what happens after the greedy 7...dxc3?

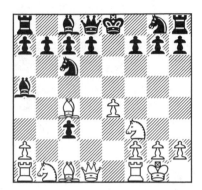

It is better to try to consolidate with on extra pawn than to hang on to two or three, and here Black learns his lesson as follows: 8 ♛b3 ♛f6 9 e5! ♛g6 10 ♘xc3 ♘ge7 11 ♗a3 0-0 12 ♖ad1 and Black is in danger of being overrun.

In the event of 7...d6 8 ♛b3 ♛f6 White also has 9 e5!?, when 9...dxe5 10 ♖e1 looks awkward for Black.

8 ♛b3

White is not interested in taking the d3-pawn when there is a juicier target in the form of the traditionally vulnerable f7-pawn.

8...♛f6 9 e5

Again.

9...♛g6 10 ♖e1 ♘ge7 11 ♗a3

It is interesting that this game is still used as a reference for this line 150 years after it was played. *NCO*, for instance, evaluates the diagram position as slightly better for White. It is easy to cancel out the two pawn deficit with White firing down the a3-f8 and a2-g8 diagonals. The territorial advantage afforded White by the e5-pawn is also

useful, and White can quickly send his queen's knight into battle with ♘b1–d2-e4 etc.

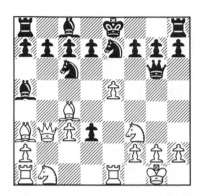

11...b5!?

Black would like to castle but 11...0-0 12 ♘bd2 followed by ♛b1, threatening ♗xd3, opens a new and potentially fruitful line for the attacker. With the text Black also gambits a pawn, serving to gain time by opening a line for his own benefit.

12 ♛xb5 ♖b8 13 ♛a4 ♗b6 14 ♘bd2 ♗b7?

Given a choice between castling and developing a queenside piece we should really do the former – particularly in a situation like this – unless there is a good reason not to. Here 14...0-0 15 ♘e4 ♔h8 has been recommended, and it is quite logical to tuck the king away in the corner. Moreover, with so many of White's pieces pointing at or around Black's king the need for shelter seems necessary according to my sense of danger which, I hope, would have set off a very loud warning bell by now.

15 ♘e4

White's queen's rook is his only outfield piece not participating in the deliberate policy of mounting the tension.

Perhaps Black should play 15...d2 here to at least distract White from his mission. Instead Black loses time with his queen.

15...♕f5? 16 ♗xd3

White would have dropped his bishop back anyway in order to harass the queen with the threat of ♘d6+.

16...♕h5 17 ♘f6+!

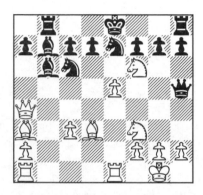

The fork forces Black to add the crucial e-file to White's already impressive list of open lines. To compound Black's predicament his forces are poorly placed to offer the king the protection it will clearly need.

17...gxf6 18 exf6 ♖g8

Hoping to make something of the g-file, the immediate threat being ...♕xf3, but the centre files are where the real action is.

19 ♖ad1! ♕xf3

19...♖g4 is the other move Anderssen had to sort out: 20 ♗c4 ♕f5 21 ♖xd7 and now Damsky in *Chess Brilliancy* gives 21...♔xd7 22 ♘e5+ ♔c8 23 ♘xg4 ♘d5 24 ♕d1 ♘d8 25 ♗d3! ♕f4 (25...♕d7 26 ♘e5) 26 ♖e4 ♘xc3 27 ♖xf4 ♘xd1 28 ♗f5+ but the recapture with the queen is even more complex: 21...♕xd7 22 ♖xe7+ ♘xe7 23 ♗xf7+ ♔xf7 24

♘e5+ ♔g8 25 f7+ ♔h8 26 ♕xd7 ♖xg2+

27 ♔f1 ♖xf2+ 28 ♔e1 ♘g6 29 ♕e8+ ♖xe8 30 fxe8♕+ ♔g7 31 ♕d7+, e.g. 31...♔g8 32 ♘g4 ♖f4 33 ♘h6+ ♔h8 34 ♘f5 or 31...♔h8 32 ♘f7+ ♔g7 (32...♔g8 33 ♘h6+ ♔h8 34 ♘f5) 33 ♘d8+ ♔g8 34 ♘e6! etc.

Damsky also gives 19...♖xg2+ 20 ♔xg2 ♘e5 21 ♕xd7+!! ♘xd7 (21...♔xd7 22 ♗g6+ or 21...♔f8 22 ♕xe7+ ♔g8 23 ♗e4) 22 ♖xe7+ ♔d8 23 ♖xd7+ ♔c8 24 ♖d8+! ♔xd8 25 ♗f5+ and mate follows.

20 ♖xe7+ ♘xe7

Black can try 20...♔d8 21 ♖xd7+ ♔c8! 22 ♖d8+ ♔xd8 (22...♘xd8 23 ♕d7+! ♔xd7 24 ♗f5+ ♔e8 25 ♗d7 mate exploits what might be called the Evans diagonal, a3-f8) 23 ♗f5+ ♕xd1+ 24 ♕xd1+ ♘d4 but White has the calm 25 g3!, e.g. 25...♖g5 26 ♗h3 ♖d5 27 cxd4 ♖xd4 28 ♕e2 and Black's king will soon be the subject of unwelcome attention once more.

21 ♕xd7+!!

Without such freedom for his pieces White would not be able to come crashing in like this. Ironically this decisive blow comes at a time when Black has a queen, rook and two raking bishops aimed at White's king.

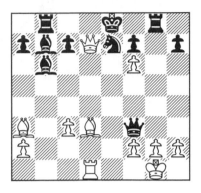

21...♔xd7 22 ♗f5+ ♔e8

22...♔c6 23 ♗d7 mate is a nice one.

23 ♗d7+ 1-0

And here is the Old Master again, this time with an even more brutal demonstration.

Rosanes-Anderssen
Breslau 1860

1 e4 e5 2 f4 d5 3 exd5 e4 4 ♗b5+

4 ♘c3 is Schulten-Morphy (Chapter 1), where 4 d3 is also briefly discussed.

4...c6

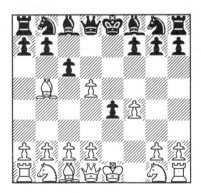

The theory is not important to us here, rather White's willingness to open lines for his opponent.

5 dxc6 ♘xc6 6 ♘c3 ♘f6 7 ♕e2 ♗c5

Having already invested a pawn for fluid development Black wastes no time defending the second. Instead he prepares to bring a rook to the e-file.

8 ♘xe4 0-0 9 ♗xc6

The immediate 9 d3? runs into 9...♘d4, and White does not want to see the royal couple exposed on the e-file. However, the text – apart from surrendering the bishop in what is quickly becoming an open position – opens the b-file for Black, a concession that White will regret.

9...bxc6 10 d3 ♖e8

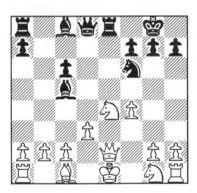

White is trying to hide away but Black enjoys too much freedom for his pieces to not find a way through enemy lines. Now the natural 11 ♘f3 ♗a6!? highlights the choices available to Black, and after 12 ♘e5, erecting another barrier, there is no holding back the tide: 12...♘xe4 13 ♕xe4 ♕d6 and ...f7-f6 is coming.

11 ♗d2 ♘xe4 12 dxe4 ♗f5 13 e5 ♕b6

White is lagging behind in development, seriously misses his light-squared bishop and has both the b2-pawn and his knight under fire. Since he is in no position to sacrifice the b-pawn, the next appears logical and best...

14 0-0-0 ♗d4

At the risk of repeating myself, do we really care that White has seven pawns to Black's five? Certainly not. The most important general feature of this position is the number of open lines at Black's disposal, allowing him to make threats across the board. White, on the other hand, finds himself at the wrong end of these lines, upon which stand too many powerful pieces.

15 c3 ♖ab8 16 b3

16 b4 invites a cheeky response in 16...♕a5! thanks to 17 bxa5 ♖b1 mate, the point being that after 17 ♔b2 Black has 17...♕xb4+ and mate.

16...♖ed8! 17 ♘f3

17 cxd4 ♕xd4 leads to mate.

17...♕xb3!

All Black's pieces have a part to play in the attack.

18 axb3 ♖xb3 19 ♗e1

Creating an escape square on d2 but, having sacrificed the mighty queen, Black has this covered.

19...♗e3+! 0-1

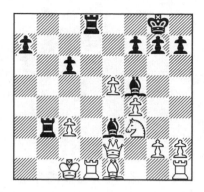

Fantastic. White seemed to be a bystander in this game, which started to go downhill as soon as he followed up the voluntary exchange of his light-squared bishop by going after the e4-pawn and consequently opening the e-file. Often a gambit might be used to open just one important file or diagonal, yet here the investments reaped rewards in the clearance of numerous lines.

A century later Spassky was pro-active in the following game – one of the best of the 1962 Olympiad in Varna. With the kings on opposite flanks, White (with a little help from his opponent) judges that the best way to open lines for an attack is to rid himself of all four kingside pawns.

Spassky-Evans
Varna Olympiad 1962

1 d4 ♘f6 2 c4 g6 3 ♘c3 ♗g7 4 e4 d6 5 f3 c6 6 ♗e3 a6 7 ♕d2 b5 8 0-0-0

White sets out his stall. We can assume that Black's king will find its way to g8 some time soon, and White wants to be ready to launch an offensive.

8...bxc4

Opening the b-file for a later attack (Black's rook will not leave a8, in fact) and introducing the idea of striking in the centre with ...d6-d5. 8...♕a5 9 ♔b1 ♘bd7 is the theoretical recommendation nowadays, with chances for both sides.

9 ♗xc4 0-0

9...♘bd7 walks into problems on the d-file after 10 e5, but Black might consider 9...d5 10 ♗b3 dxe4 11 fxe4 ♘g4, although such active play in these positions can be risky when underdeveloped.

10 h4!

Wasting no time.

10...d5

10...h5 is an option but I can understand Black's decision to hold back in order not to weaken the g6-pawn (note that the f7-pawn is pinned) and to avoid the close quarter combat that will follow a well timed g2-g4 etc.

10...♗e6 is a suggestion of Petrosian. Contesting the a2-g8 diagonal makes sense but probably not at the cost of leaving the light squares in front of Black's king susceptible to attack after ♗xe6 ...fxe6 etc. Had Petrosian's name

not been tagged on to ...♗e6 I guess I would hardly have considered it.

11 ♗b3 dxe4 12 h5!

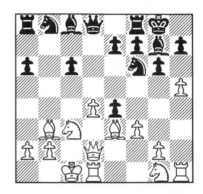

Again time is a more important factor than material in this rather urgent situation. 12 fxe4 ♘g4 or 12...♗g4 13 ♘f3 ♘bd7 looks too comfortable for Black.

12...exf3

Not an easy decision to make when the enemy is approaching. After 12...♘xh5 13 g4 ♘f6 White can continue the offensive with 14 ♗h6 or 14 ♕h2, while 13 ♗h6 followed by 14 ♖xh5 gxh5 15 ♕g5 or 14 ♘xe4 has been proposed.

13 hxg6 hxg6 14 ♗h6 fxg2

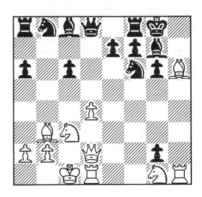

Black removes the final kingside pawn (note that all four of his own remain in play). Consequently White has a fully open file for his exclusive use and no difficulty when the time comes to transfer the appropriate pieces to the kingside to join in the attack. The bishop still reigns supreme on the a2-g8 diagonal, pinning the f7-pawn and therefore removing the protection from g6.

15 ♖h4

White plans to exchange bishops on g7 and wade in on h6. A mistake would be 15 ♕xg2 because after 15...♗g4! the fact that the queen no longer has access to h6 gives Black the opportunity to put up a much needed barrier on the h-file with ...♗h5.

15...♘g4

Trying to block with 15...♘h5 loses to 16 ♖xh5 gxh5 17 ♕g5, a standard theme in this kind of attack.

16 ♗xg7 ♔xg7 17 ♕xg2

17...♘h6

The knight heads for the defensive post on f5. Since White has let two pawns go, each of Black's options requires some consideration: 17...♘e3? doesn't look right – 18 ♕h2! ♖h8 (18...♘xd1 19 ♖h7+ mates) 19 ♖xh8 ♕xh8 20 ♕e5+ picks up the knight.

17...♘f6 is best met with the simple 18 ♘f3, intending ♖dh1, or ♘e5 followed by ♗xf7 etc. Then 18...♖h8 19 ♗xf7! looks strong, e.g. 19...♔xf7 20 ♘e5+ ♔e6 21 ♕h3+ ♔d6 22 ♘f7+

22...♔c7 23 ♕g3+ and the end is nigh.

Giving up two useful looking pieces for a rook in order to contest the h-file merely leaves White free to make his presence felt elsewhere: 17...♖h8 18 ♖xg4 ♗xg4 19 ♕xg4 ♘d7 20 ♘f3 ♘f6 21 ♕f4 and ♘e5 is coming.

17...f5 is brave but compromises the kingside more than Black can afford after 18 ♘f3 ♖h8 19 ♖xh8 ♕xh8 20 ♖h1 ♕d8 21 ♘g5 and matters have grown even worse for Black.

The lesser evil might be 17...♕d6 18 ♖xg4 ♗xg4 19 ♕xg4 f5 20 ♕g5 ♕f6 21 ♘f3 ♘d7 with a rook and two pawns for bishop and knight.

18 ♘f3 ♘f5 19 ♖h2

The knight has arrived on f5, free from any pawn attacks, defending h6 and generally keeping an eye on White. However, Black might as well forget about his two pawn lead since he needs to channel his energies on survival and, with so many of White's forces pointing in the direction of his king, this might well be futile.

19...♕d6

19...♘e3? 20 ♕g5! and 19...♖h8 20 ♗xf7! are in the air, and 19...e6 20 ♘g5 also looks good for White. With 19...♘d7 20 ♖dh1 ♘f6 Black quickly sends the other knight over but only to witness the end in 21 ♗xf7! ♔xf7 22 ♘e5+ ♔e6 23 ♕xc6+ etc.

20 ♘e5 ♘d7

20...♘xd4 is asking for trouble, e.g. 21 ♕g5!, while 20...♗e6 21 ♘e4 turns the screw.

21 ♘e4 ♕c7 22 ♖dh1

It is a very promising sign when every piece is involved in the attack. Having lured Black's d-pawn on a journey that saw it take the route ...d6-d5xe4xf3xg2, White enjoys an unobstructed diagonal for his bishop (an important feature) and a clear enough view of Black's defences for his queen and rooks. Meanwhile the knights do their collective octopus impression in the middle of the board. Black's next is aimed at providing the g6-pawn with protection.

22...♖g8

22...♘f6 23 ♗xf7! is a decisive breakthrough.

23 ♖h7+ ♔f8 24 ♖xf7+ ♔e8 25 ♕xg6!

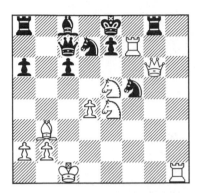

This queen 'sacrifice' sees each of White's major pieces operating an open file, working well with the other forces.

25...♘xe5 26 ♖f8+ 1-0

A fitting finish.

The final game in our section on open lines features the Closed Variation of the Catalan Opening. This is an opening favoured by top GMs, being flexible, rich in possibilities and quite suitable for different styles of play, yet it is often perceived by club players as boring (they don't know what they're missing). Hopefully this display might attract more adherents to the Catalan...

Spassky-Ciric
Amsterdam 1970

1 d4 d5 2 c4 e6 3 ♘f3 ♘f6 4 g3 ♗e7 5 ♗g2 0-0 6 0-0

White responds to the QGD not with the 'natural' development of his light-squared bishop on, for example, the d3-square but instead with a fianchetto. Should Black take on c4 the bishop will enjoy considerable scope on the long diagonal – indeed there are a number of gambit lines where White builds an imposing territorial supremacy and active pieces while Black is busy hanging on to the c4-pawn. Alternatively, Black can follow Ciric's strategy in this game, namely setting up a very solid centre, behind which he can complete development in preparation for a tense middlegame.

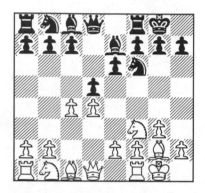

6...c6 7 b3 ♘bd7 8 ♗b2

The old 'hypermodern' school of thought is popular today. If the centre pawns are cleared away White's bishops will criss-cross the board, between them covering a number of key squares.

8...b6 9 ♘bd2 ♗b7 10 ♖c1 ♖c8

The constructive shadow-boxing

continues, with both players improving their forces without making a premature commitment.

11 e3

Also possible is 11 ♘e5, White finally sending a piece passed the fourth rank. Then 11...♘xe5 12 dxe5 ♘d7 13 e4 steps up the pace in the centre, but Black does best to hold steady with 13...♘c5 with an unclear position, putting the onus on White to act on the stand-off that revolves around d5.

11...c5

After developing within the confines of their respective territories thus far, the players suddenly meet in the middle of the board, with four pawns face-to-face. Just to add to the tension, the position is completely symmetrical, so something must give sooner or later. Ironically both patience and initiative are two important characteristics here, for losing the former and being afraid to go for the latter could have serious consequences. Instead of the text Black tends to prefer going his own way here with 11...dxc4, when 12 ♘xc4 is best met with 12...b5 13 ♘ce5 a6 with an interesting struggle ahead, rather than 12...c5 13 ♕e2 when White's lead in development leaves him better able to deal with the inevitable opening of the position.

12 ♕e2

A significant difference in the diagram position is the respective freedom of the queens. The e2-square is a good post because from here the queen can keep in touch with all sectors of the board, but c7 is far from ideal for Black's queen in view of the enemy rook sharing the c-file. With this in mind Black's next makes way for the queen to take up residence on a8, supporting the bishop and making way for the king's rook.

12...♖c7 13 cxd5 ♗xd5

13...exd5 gives the game a different flavour. With a potential weakness fixed on d5 most players would prefer to be sitting on White's side of the board, but ...exd5 does help both monitor the e4-square and support an outpost there, while Black can also look forward to using the half-open e-file.

14 e4 ♗b7 15 e5

White's would-be initiative gains momentum.

15...♘d5 16 ♘c4 ♕a8 17 ♘d6!

And here, finally, is the gambit! Over the last few moves the game has begun to open up considerably, particularly the h1–a8 diagonal. At the moment neither side can make anything of this because the bishops cancel each other out, but with the aggressive text the knight jumps into the heart of Black's position to threaten to eliminate the light-squared bishop, after which White would rule the priceless long diagonal. Consequently Black needs to address this issue, and 17...♗c6 18 dxc5 leaves

Black with either broken (and therefore weak) pawns after 18...bxc5 or problems with the important bishop after 18...♘xc5 19 ♘d4 etc. This means that Black's next is practically forced.

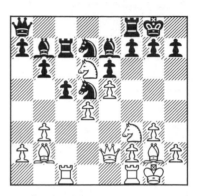

17...♗xd6

Unfortunately for Black this capture not only parts with a bishop for knight in a position that looks like opening up in the near future but, to add to Black's problems, the recapture on d6 helps clear the other long diagonal for White's hitherto quiet bishop.

18 exd6 ♖c6 19 dxc5 bxc5

After 19...♘xc5 20 ♘g5! White gets busy on the kingside.

20 ♘g5!

Quite a transformation. With his

bishops suddenly promoted to powerful, long-range pieces White is happy to gambit the d6-pawn. Only the rook on f1 is missing out on the action, with all the other pieces enjoying plenty of scope. Meanwhile, Black now needs to address the threat of ♘xe6.

20...♖xd6 21 ♖fd1

White's compensation is wonderful, with open lines for all the relevant pieces.

21...♖a6

Due to the new pin on the d-file 21...♘7f6 runs into 22 ♗xf6, when 22...gxf6 23 ♕h5! fxg5 24 ♕xg5+ ♔h8 25 ♕e5+ picks up the unfortunate rook. 21...h6 is a natural reaction to the arrival of the knight. Then 22 ♘e4 ♖a6 23 ♕g4 puts the b2-bishop to good use by threatening mate on g7, and 23...f6 24 ♘xc5 ♘xc5 25 ♖xc5 nets a pawn for nothing. Note that 25...♘e3? rebounds on Black after 26 fxe3 ♗xg2 27 ♖d7 ♖f7 28 ♖xf7 ♔xf7 29 ♖c7+ etc.

22 ♕e4! f5

22...♘7f6 fails to 23 ♗xf6 thanks to the pin on the knight. 22...g6 blocks one diagonal but completely clears away another, inviting the decisive 23 ♘xh7!

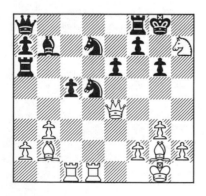

This is a standard theme in this kind

of situation and is the culmination of White's gambit play.

23 ♕c4

Threatening ♘xe6.

23...♕e8 24 ♖e1

Switching the focus of his attention to the e-file, White is happy to let the a2-pawn go.

24...♖xa2

24...♔h8 loses to 25 ♗xd5 exd5 26 ♖xe8 dxc4 27 ♖e7, while 24...♖b6 is punished by 25 ♖xe6! ♖xe6 26 ♗xd5 ♗xd5 27 ♕xd5 etc.

25 ♖xe6 ♕a8 26 ♗xd5 ♗xd5 27 ♕h4 h6 28 ♕xh6!

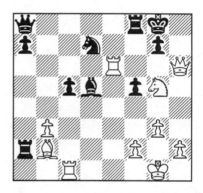

Spot the irony. Black is about to lose the game just as he has acquired sole ownership of the Catalan diagonal. The important action is taking place on the other long diagonal, where a nice mate would appear after 28...gxh6 29 ♖g6.

28...♘f6 29 ♖xf6! 1-0

Black threw in the towel because mate in one is threatened and taking the queen results in the same mate, while a sample finish is 29...♖xf6 30 ♕h7+ ♔f8 31 ♕h8+ ♔e7 (31...♗g8 32 ♗xf6) 32 ♕xg7+ ♖f7 33 ♘xf7 ♗h1 (33...♗xf7 34 ♖e1+) 34 ♘e5+.

CHAPTER THREE

The Initiative

The initiative is surprisingly under-used in chess. We are often afraid to fight for it, or we might have difficulty actually exploiting the activity an initiative affords and the pressure the opposition experiences as the tension mounts. An initiative that results from a gambit tends to be easier to play, not least because the material imbalance injects the game with a sense of urgency that is impossible to ignore. The attraction of winning a pawn or two tempts the defender into making concessions that otherwise he might not have contemplated, thus adding weight to the initiative. Two of the examples in this chapter feature Kasparov, whose thirst for activity sees him wrest the initiative from the opposition as Black as often as other top players fight with White.

Yudasin-Kasparov
Ljubljana 1995

1 e4 c5 2 ♘f3 d6 3 ♗b5+

This system, that has less bite than against 2...♘c6, is mainly employed as a means of containing aggressive players

– a particularly appropriate strategy when facing Kasparov.

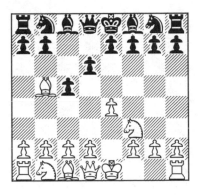

3...♘d7

The most 'active' block, despite appearances. Black refuses to exchange bishops and plans to gain time on the bishop later with ...a7-a6.

4 d4 ♘gf6 5 ♘c3 cxd4 6 ♕xd4 e5

Played by a beginner, we might think of criticising this thrust, which creates a backward pawn on d6 and the traditional hole on d5. However, Black seems to get away with this more often in the Sicilian than in other defences and, as we are about to see, Kasparov has a special role in mind for the d-pawn.

7 ♕d3 h6

Preventing a second pin with ♗g5. Thus far Black is lagging behind in development, but there are no pawn breaks and the position is not really open, so White cannot exploit his lead.

8 ♘d2

Heading for c4, from where the knight will both attack the d6-pawn and be ready to drop back to e3 to clamp down on d5.

8...♗e7 9 ♘c4 0-0

Ignoring the 'threat' to take on d6 which, on the next move, loses after 10 ♘xd6? ♘c5.

10 ♗xd7 ♗xd7!

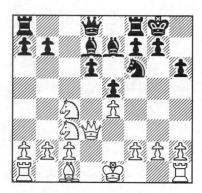

In the space of a few moves we see that Black is now closer to completing development and White has parted with his light-squared bishop, while the weakness on d6 remains, and in turn the accompanying hole on d5. Sitting on White's side of the board in the diagram position, it is interesting to consider how we would react to the offer of the d6-pawn. After all, White has sent his knight around to c4 in order to attack it. And should Yudasin be less inclined to accept the gambit because the resulting

compensation might be more dangerous than usual in the hands of Gazza? Play the position or play the man? I suppose that, when in doubt, playing the position is the sensible, confident course, which prompted White to make the following decision.

11 ♘xd6?!

Taking up the challenge (and not wishing to give the impression of being afraid, of being psyched out). However, the more circumspect, positionally oriented 11 ♘e3 is preferable, using the 'extra' knight to leave Black with the long-term weakness on d6 (which White might later attack). Then 11...♗e6 12 0-0 ♖c8 is given as equal by Kasparov.

11...♕c7 12 ♘f5

12 ♘db5 ♕c6 looks rather awkward for White.

12...♗xf5 13 exf5 e4

Black continues in aggressive fashion. Also effective is 13...♖fd8!?, when the attempt by White to counter with 14 ♕g3? can be ignored: 14...♕c4! 15 ♗xh6 (15 b3 ♕a6) 15...♘h5 16 ♕f3 gxh6 17 ♕xh5 ♗b4 18 ♕f3 ♖d4

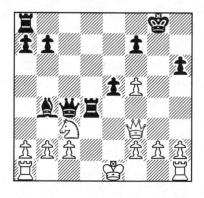

Black's kingside has been damaged but it is White who has defensive problems because his king is stuck in the centre. Meanwhile the other rook is ready to come to d8. Once again the two extra pawns are quite irrelevant here. Better is 14 ♕e2 ♗b4 15 0-0 (15 ♗d2? ♖xd2! 16 ♔xd2 ♘d5) 15...♗xc3 16 bxc3 ♕xc3 17 ♖b1 b6, when 18 ♖b3 has been assessed as unclear (White has the potentially superior minor piece, Black the superior structure), and 18 ♗b2 ♖d2 as favouring Black.

14 ♘xe4?!

Kasparov gives 14 ♕h3? ♕c4 as clearly better for Black. Taking on e4 was a theoretical novelty at the time, but Kasparov's appendix of '?!' suggests Yudasin's idea is inferior to the known 14 ♕e2.

14...♕e5

Better than 14...♗b4+? 15 c3 ♘xe4 16 cxb4 ♖ad8 17 ♕b3 with advantage to White (not 17 ♕e2? ♘c3!).

15 f3

When lagging behind in development and on the wrong side of the initiative we should be wary of tactics that seem to work in our favour. An example here is 15 0-0? ♘xe4 (15...♕xe4? 16 ♕xe4 ♘xe4 17 ♖e1) 16 ♖e1 ♖ad8

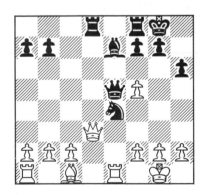

White's vulnerable back rank rules out the capture on e4. This situation is symptomatic of White's general predicament which, due to Black's dangerous initiative, is susceptible to quickly going downhill in the event of even slightly inaccurate play.

15...♖ad8

Obvious, best and giving White another opportunity to go wrong.

16 ♕c3

16 ♕e2? looks natural but works out badly for White after 16...♘xe4, e.g. 17 ♕xe4 ♗h4+! 18 g3 (18 ♔e2? ♖fe8 is decisive) 18...♗xg3+ 19 ♔f1 (19 hxg3 ♕xg3+ spells the end) 19...♗xh2, or (worse) 17 fxe4 ♗b4+ 18 ♔f2 ♖d4 19 ♔f3 ♖e8 20 ♗f4 ♕e7, when 21 e5? runs into 21...♖xf4+! 22 ♔xf4 ♕g5+ 23 ♔f3 (23 ♔e4 ♖xe5+ 24 ♔xe5 ♕e7+) 23...♕xf5+ 24 ♔g3 ♖xe5

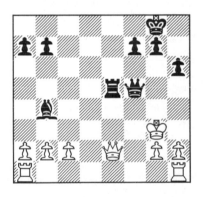

Black's initiative has reaped rewards. As is often the case when the defender has had no time to put up a fight, White's rooks remain rooted to their corner posts.

16...♕xf5 17 0-0

Having returned one of the gambit pawns, White is relieved to hand back the other if it means being able to get his king safe, which would not be the case after 17 ♘xf6+ ♗xf6, for example.

17...♘xe4 18 fxe4 ♕xe4

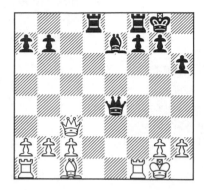

Material is level but Black still retains a pull thanks to his more active forces. Consequently Kasparov is able to maintain some kind of momentum, so White can by no means relax.

19 ♗e3

19 ♖e1 is a mistake in view of 19...♗c5+! 20 ♔h1 ♕h4 etc. The text secures the g1–a7 diagonal while connecting the rooks.

19...a6

Black must also be careful if he is to make something of what is left of the initiative. For example 19...♗f6?! invites 20 ♖xf6! gxf6 21 ♗xh6 ♖fe8 22 ♕xf6 ♕d4+ when the game is balanced. Similarly, White's structural downside after 19...♖c8?! 20 ♕d3 ♕xd3 21 cxd3 a6 is not enough to confer upon Black an advantage after 22 ♖ac1, according to Kasparov. The text is a sensible and safe move that retains the tension and puts the onus on White to continue what has thus far been a decent display since bravely accepting the gambit(s).

20 ♖f4?!

It is interesting that such 'aggressive' play tends to follow a quiet move in these situations in which the player gradually getting back into the game wants to make his presence felt. Kasparov proposes 20 ♕b3!, monitoring the b7-pawn and removing the queen from a potentially awkward dark square. Yudasin's choice, on the other hand, makes life a little more difficult for White because yet another piece lands on this colour complex, on which Black's bishop is better placed to operate than its opposite number.

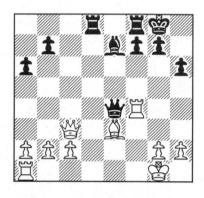

20...♕g6 21 ♖f2 ♗h4! 22 g3

22 ♖d2 ♖xd2 23 ♕xd2 ♖d8 allows Black to mobilise and again take up a menacing stance.

22...♗f6 23 ♕b4?!

Again Kasparov prefers 23 ♕b3.

23...♖fe8 24 ♗b6 ♖d5 25 a4 h5!

With White's kingside beginning to creak, Kasparov smells blood. Black's forces work well together, which cannot be said for White, whose rook is the king's only friend at the moment, and poorly placed on f2. Remember that White put in considerable effort earlier, returning both gambit pawns to diffuse Black's initiative. Unfortunately the flames were not put out altogether, and now the fire threatens to engulf White once more.

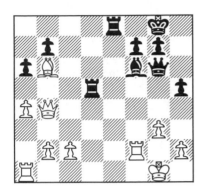

26 ♕b3 ♖de5! 27 ♖af1 h4! 28 ♔h1 ♖e1

Black closes in.

29 a5

Kasparov gives 29 gxh4 ♖8e2 30 ♕h3 (30 ♕g3 ♕e4+ 31 ♔g1 ♖xf1+ 32 ♖xf1 ♗e5) 30...♗e5 31 ♖xe2 ♕c6+ 32 ♔g1 ♖xe2 etc.

29...h3

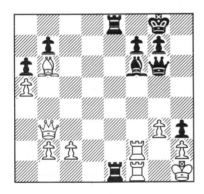

The last few moves emphasise the potentially negative implications of a kingside pawn minority. Without means of effective counterplay, any weakness is liable to trigger an aggressive response from the opposition, whose extra pawn often affords a certain measure of flexibility (and security) in terms of launching an offensive. In this case

White had to deal with the prospect of ...h4xg3 in some lines, while marching on to h3 is equally troublesome for the defender.

30 ♕f3

30 ♕d3 ♕xd3 31 cxd3 ♖xf1+ 32 ♖xf1 ♗xb2 will prove untenable for White, while 30 ♕c4 ♖xf1+ 31 ♕xf1 ♗xb2 32 ♕xh3 manages to pick up the problem pawn but pays too big a price after 32...♖e1+ 33 ♖f1 ♕e4+ 34 ♔g1 ♗d4+ 35 ♗xd4 ♕xd4+ 36 ♔h1 ♕d5+ 37 ♔g1 ♕c5+ 38 ♔h1 ♖xf1+ 39 ♕xf1 ♕xa5 etc.

30...♖xf1+ 31 ♖xf1 ♕xc2 32 ♕xb7 ♖e4!

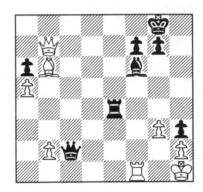

Very nice.

33 ♖g1

If 33 ♗f2 then 33...♗d4 wins for Black, but 33...♕xf2?, while appearing to win on the spot, allows White to fight on with the surprising continuation 34 ♕c8+ ♗d8 35 ♕xd8+ ♔h7 36 ♕h4+! etc.

33...♖e2 0-1

After accepting Kasparov's gambit with 11 ♘xd6?! White struggled to survive, the brief period of near stability soon giving way to renewed pressure. A typical Kasparov display.

The next game sees the acceptance of White's gambit pawns result in an immediate kingside attack.

V.Ivanov-Losev
Moscow Championship 1995

1 e4 c5 2 c3 ♘f6 3 e5 ♘d5 4 d4 cxd4 5 ♘f3 e6 6 cxd4 b6 7 ♘c3 ♗b7 8 ♗d3 ♗e7 9 0-0 0-0 10 ♕e2

Black's bishop is actively posted on b7 but White's set-up is perfectly suited for a kingside attack.

10...♘xc3

An attempted improvement on the previously favoured continuation which was 10...f5. Vladimir Ivanov investigates 10...f6!?, offering 11 ♘xd5 ♗xd5 12 ♗e4 ♗xe4 13 ♕xe4 ♘c6 14 exf6 ♗xf6 15 d5 exd5 16 ♕xd5+ ♔h8 17 ♗g5 with a slight but enduring advantage to White in the shape of the isolated d-pawn.

11 bxc3 d6 12 exd6! ♕xd6

Black must be careful here. 12...♗xd6? promotes the bishop to a more promising diagonal but neglects the g5-square, inviting 13 ♘g5 with a menacing attack brewing.

13 a4!

White can also make his presence felt on the other flank, the text threatening to undermine Black's cosy queenside duo. Instead the natural 13 ♘g5 works out well for White after 13...♗xg5?! 14 ♗xg5 ♗xg2 (14...♕d5 15 ♕g4) 15 ♔xg2 ♕d5+ 16 ♗e4! (16 ♕e4? ♗xg5+ 17 ♔h1 ♕d5) 16...♕xg5+ 17 ♔h1. However, 13...h6 14 ♘h7 ♖c8! is much less clear, e.g. 15 ♕g4 ♔h8! 16 ♕h5 ♖xc3 17 ♗xh6

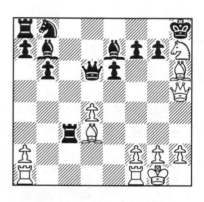

White is throwing a great deal into the attack but it will fail: 17...♖xd3 18 ♕xf7 ♕xd4 (18...gxh6 19 ♘f6 ♗xf6 20 ♕xf6+ ♔h7 21 ♕f7+ draws) 19 ♕xe7 ♕d7 etc.

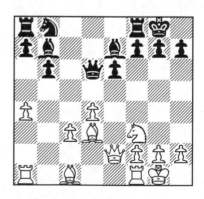

13...♕c7?!

13...♘c6 14 ♘g5 ♗xg5 (14...h6 15

♕e4 g6 compromises Black's defensive wall and is difficult for the defender after 16 ♘f3 ♔g7 17 ♕e3 ♖h8 18 ♗b2) 15 ♗xg5 favours the bishop pair but is nevertheless preferable for Black to the text.

14 ♘g5

Perhaps Black believed that his last move effectively prevented this aggression in view of the attack on the c3-pawn.

14...♗xg5

Now 14...h6 15 ♘h7! ♖d8 is different after 16 ♕g4

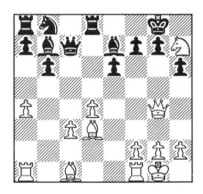

Then 16...♔h8 17 ♕h3 (planning ♗xh6) 17...♕c6 18 ♘g5! looks strong, e.g. 18...♔g8 19 ♗h7+! ♔f8 20 ♗e4 ♕c7 21 ♕f3! with a crushing double attack on b7 and f7, or 18...♖f8 19 ♗e4 ♕c7 20 ♕f3! ♗xe4 21 ♕xe4 f5 22 ♘xe6 etc. The lesser evil is 18...♗xg5 19 ♗xg5 ♕xg2+ 20 ♕xg2 ♗xg2 21 ♔xg2 hxg5 22 ♗e4, albeit still rather difficult for Black.

Returning to the diagram position, 16...g6 runs into 17 ♗xg6!, but with 16...f5 Black might be able to limit White to an edge, e.g. 17 ♕g6 ♕c6 18 f3.

15 ♗xg5 ♕xc3?

Part of Black's plan, it seems, but a seriously faulty one. Necessary is 15...♘d7 16 ♕e3 ♖fc8 17 ♖ac1 when White's bishop enjoy good scope but at least Black is well in the game. This is not the case after the gambit.

16 ♖ac1! ♕xd4

16...♕a5 17 ♗b5! introduces the threat of ♗d2, trapping the queen. In the event of 17...♕b4 there comes 18 ♖c7 followed by the decisive ♗e7, which leaves 17...♗a6 18 ♗e7 ♖e8 19 ♖c7, e.g. 19...♗xb5 20 axb5 a6 21 ♕f3 axb5 22 ♗b4! and Black suffers again thanks to his queen.

17 ♖fd1!

Better than the obvious 17 ♖c4 ♕d5 18 ♗e4 ♕xg5 19 ♗xb7 ♘d7 20 ♗xa8 ♖xa8 when Black's sound structure and two pawns for the exchange are significant.

17...♕xa4 18 ♖c4!

This time the rook comes to c4 with an altogether different purpose, for now it is the enemy king that will be the target of White's suddenly unhindered forces. Black's pawn grabbing spree with his queen has served only to transform a 'chances for both sides' situation into one in which Black's kingside is about to be overrun. White's gambit went from one to three pawns and, during the time it took for Black's queen to take them – culminating in a ridiculously isolated location way over on the queenside – White has been able to fully mobilise his forces.

18...♕a5

18...♕b5 places the queen on a diagonal 'owned' by White, and is duly punished after 19 ♗xh7+! ♔xh7 20 ♖h4+ and 21 ♕xb5.

19 ♕h5?

As the tension mounts White risks spoiling a superb gambit display. Correct is 19 ♗xh7+! ♔xh7 20 ♕h5+ ♔g8 21 ♖h4

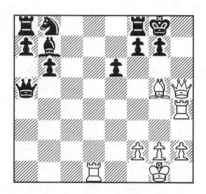

Now Black must move the f-pawn. In response to 21...f6 White finishes with 22 ♕h7+ ♔f7 23 ♗h6 ♖g8 24 ♖g4, while 21...f5 22 ♗f6!! ♖xf6 23 ♖d8+ ♖f8 24 ♕h8+ is curtains for Black.

19...h6?

Returning the favour. 19...g6! creates holes on the dark squares but is the remedy. Then Ivanov gives 20 ♕h6 ♕e5! 21 ♖c7! ♗d5 (21...♕xc7? 22 ♗f6) 22 ♗b5! with the threat of 23 ♕xf8+! ♔xf8 24 ♗h6+ ♔g8 25 ♖c8 mate.

Forced is 22...♕g7 23 ♕h4 h5 24 ♗e7 a6 25 ♗xf8 ♕xf8 26 ♖dc1 axb5 27 ♖c8 ♘c6 28 ♖xf8+ ♖xf8 which Ivanov assesses as equal. The important difference between ...g7-g6 and the text is that the former is structurally more solid.

20 ♖g4 ♖d8?

20...♔h8 walks into 21 ♕xh6+! gxh6 22 ♗f6 mate. 20...♘d7 meets with the cheeky 21 ♗f6!! ♘xf6 (21...♕xh5 22 ♖xg7+ ♔h8 23 ♖h7+ ♔g8 24 ♖h8 mate) 22 ♕xh6. White also finds a way in against 20...f5 21 ♗xh6 fxg4 22 ♕g6, e.g. 22...♕e5 (22...♖f7 23 ♗xg7!) 23 ♕h7+ ♔f7 24 ♗g6+ ♔e7 25 ♗xg7.

In the event of 20...♖e8 Ivanov gives 21 ♗h7+(!) ♔xh7 (21...♔f8 22 ♖f4) 22 ♕xf7 but then 22...♕f5 wins for Black. However, instead of 21 ♗h7+? White has 21 ♕xh6! gxh6 22 ♗xh6+ ♔h8 23 ♗g7+ ♔g8 24 ♗f6+ ♔f8 25 ♗h7

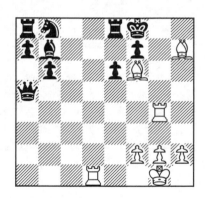

Finally there is 20...f6 21 ♕g6 fxg5 (21...hxg5 22 ♕h7+ ♔f7 23 ♗g6+ ♔e7 24 ♕xg7+) 22 ♕xe6+ ♔h8 23 ♕g6 ♔g8 24 ♕h7+ ♔f7 25 ♗c4+ ♔f6 26 ♖d6+ ♔e7 27 ♕xg7+ ♔xd6 28 ♖d4+ ♔c6 (28...♔c5 29 ♕e5+ ♔b4 30 ♗d5+) 29 ♕g6+ etc. In each of these variations White's attack is made possible by the rapid mobilisation that results from the gambit of the centre pawns.

21 ♗f6!! 1-0

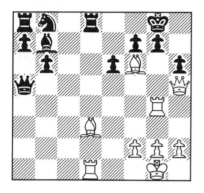

This must have been satisfying to play. Now 21...♕xh5 22 ♗h7+! is final, e.g. 22...♔xh7 23 ♖xg7+ ♔h8 24 ♖xd8 mate, or 22...♔h8 23 ♖xd8+ ♔xh7 24 ♖xg7 mate. Nor does 21...♖xd3 slow White down thanks to 22 ♖xg7+.

This was one of those gambits which seems foolhardy to accept, yet Black (over 2300 FIDE) obliged.

The 'latest' theory doesn't always revolve around modern openings, and fashion – as in life – can often be influenced by the choices of the world's top GMs. The following game, where Kasparov blows away one of the era's greatest talents, helped bring the romantic Evans Gambit back into the international fold.

Kasparov-Anand
Riga 1995

1 e4 e5 2 ♘f3 ♘c6 3 ♗c4 ♗c5 4 b4 ♗xb4

Black almost always accepts this particular gambit. Dropping back with 4...♗b6 anyway permits White to continue in uncompromising style if he so wishes: 5 a4 a6 6 ♘c3 ♘f6 7 ♘d5 ♘xd5 8 exd5 ♘d4 9 a5 ♗a7 10 d6!? and White puts his faith in easier development.

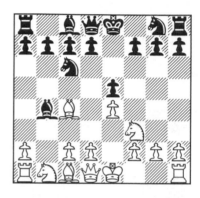

5 c3 ♗e7

5...♗c5 6 d4 and 5...♗a5 6 0-0 are the major alternatives.

6 d4 ♘a5

6...exd4 7 ♕b3 ♘a5 8 ♗xf7+ ♔f8 9 ♕a4 ♔xf7 10 ♕xa5 provides White with obvious compensation for the gambit (Black's king), but Black should avoid 6...d6 7 ♕b3.

7 ♗e2!?

An interesting alternative to 7 ♘xe5, when 7...♘xc4 8 ♘xc4 d5 9 exd5 ♕xd5

10 ♘e3 followed by 0-0, c3-c4 and easy development favours White. Kasparov's choice concentrates on the centre and on the kingside in that Black's knight might prove quite poor over on a5.

7...exd4

7...♘f6? runs into 8 dxe5 ♘xe4 9 ♕a4, but 7...d6 8 ♕a4+ c6 9 dxe5 dxe5 10 ♘xe5 ♘f6 11 0-0 is a shade better for White.

8 ♕xd4!

The point, and Kasparov's improvement on 8 cxd4?! ♘f6. By recapturing with the queen White abandons any plans of establishing a pawn centre in favour of drumming up an early initiative, the development advantage and extra space facilitating an offensive.

8...♘f6?!

The '?!' is awarded by Kasparov, who offers 8...♔f8, 8...f6 and the interesting 8...d5. In Shirov-Timman, Biel 1995 Black fought to stay in the game with a gambit of his own: 8...d6!? 9 ♕xg7 ♗f6 10 ♕g3 ♕e7 11 0-0 offering chances to both sides.

9 e5 ♘c6 10 ♕h4 ♘d5 11 ♕g3

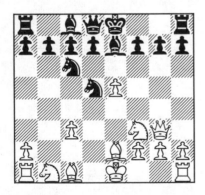

Anand's strategy has seen his knights take up residence in the centre but now his kingside comes under fire. White's territorial supremacy afforded him by the e5-pawn is a major factor, making the initiative all the more potent.

11...g6

After 11...0-0?! 12 ♗h6 g6 Kasparov suggests ignoring the rook, exploiting White's attacking chances instead with the no-nonsense 13 h4.

12 0-0

White has a slight advantage according to Kasparov.

12...♘b6

Black loses more time with his knights. This time 12...0-0 13 ♗h6 ♖e8 14 c4 ♘b6 15 ♘c3 d6 16 ♖ad1 is awkward for Black, Kasparov continuing 16...♘d7 17 ♘g5! dxe5 (17...♘dxe5 18 f4) 18 f4 with a clear advantage to White. White has obvious compensation after 12...d6 13 ♖d1 etc.

13 c4 d6

13...d5 14 cxd5 ♕xd5 15 ♘c3 seems to help White as much as Black, but Kasparov's suggestion of 13...♘a4!? – ironically – might be best.

14 ♖d1 ♘d7

14...♗e6 15 c5 illustrates the point of Black's last which, unfortunately, leaves him rather cramped.

15 ♗h6!

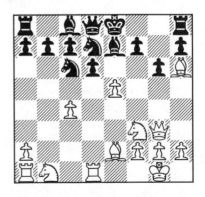

Consistent. The e5-pawn has served its purpose, and White is more interested in concentrating his efforts on the plight of Black's king.

15...♘cxe5

Black wants e5 for a knight, and the text seems preferable to 15...dxe5 16 ♘c3 ♗f8 17 ♗g5, e.g. 17...f6 18 ♗e3 ♗g7 19 c5 0-0 20 ♗c4+ ♔h8 21 ♘h4! ♘e7 (21...♕e8 22 ♘b5) 22 ♘d5 ♘xd5 23 ♘xg6+! hxg6 24 ♗xd5, or 17...♗e7 18 ♘d5 ♗xg5 19 ♘xg5 h6 (19...0-0 20 ♕h4 h5 21 ♗xh5) 20 ♘e6!

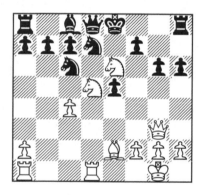

Note the contrasting roles of the knights here. 20...fxe6 21 ♕xg6+ ♔f8 22 ♗h5 ends the game.

16 ♘xe5 ♘xe5

16...dxe5 is even worse this time in view of 17 ♘c3 ♗f8 18 ♖xd7! and ♕xe5+ etc.

17 ♘c3

17 ♗g7?! is not in the spirit of White's energetic gambit approach, 17...♗f6 18 ♗xh8 ♗xh8 19 ♘c3 b6 being far from clear, but 17 c5!? deserves a look.

17...f6

Anand disturbs the f-pawn on his own terms. Otherwise 17...♘d7 18 ♘e4! continues to add pressure, e.g.

18...f5 19 ♘g5 ♘c5 20 ♗f3, or 18...♗f8 19 ♕c3 f6 20 ♗f4! (Kasparov).

18 c5!

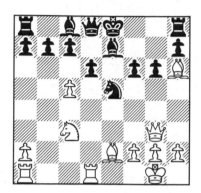

Chipping away once more. Black cannot be allowed to regroup with a solid set-up. The initiative is an animal that requires constant attention if it is to fulfil its potential and bring the best results, so White makes sure to get the most from it here, his latest seeking to undermine Black's centre to add to his problems on the kingside.

18...♘f7 19 cxd6 cxd6

In the event of 19...♗xd6 20 ♗b5+ c6 (20...♗d7 21 ♖e1+) 21 ♗f4 cxb5 22 ♗xd6 ♘xd6 23 ♖xd6 Black is in no position to properly defend.

20 ♕e3! ♘xh6

20...♕b6 21 ♗b5+ is poor for Black after either 21...♗d7 22 ♗xd7+ ♔xd7 23 ♕h3+ f5 24 ♘d5 or 21...♔d8 22 ♕e2 ♘xh6 23 ♘d5 etc.

21 ♕xh6 ♗f8 22 ♕e3+!

22 ♗b5+?! is tempting but White's queen is attacked, remember, so that after 22...♔f7 23 ♗c4+ d5! White must retreat with 24 ♕h4 (24 ♖xd5 ♗xh6 25 ♖xd8+ ♔g7), when 24...♔g7 25 ♘xd5 ♗d6 sees Black begin to get back into the game.

22...♔f7 23 ♘d5

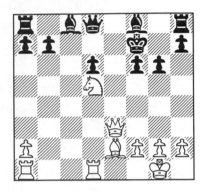

24 ♘f4 ♛e7 25 ♖e1! 1-0

This is one of those 'the smoke has cleared' positions, the crucial point being that this does not mean Black is out of trouble. Instead White's initiative has been transformed into an overall domination of the centre which, combined with his far superior forces, guarantees at least a clear advantage. Moreover, Black's only 'developed' piece is his king, and will be a while until the rest of his pieces see the light of day. This compounds the defensive task considerably.

23...♗e6?!

An understandable mistake under pressure – even for one of the world's top players. Nor does the otherwise desirable 23...♗g7 help Black in view of 24 ♗c4 ♗e6 25 ♗b3!, the idea behind dropping the bishop back to b3 to threaten ♘f4, when ...♗xb3 allows a devastating recapture with the queen. After 25...♖e8 26 ♘f4 d5 27 ♘xe6 ♖xe6 28 ♖xd5! Black's nightmare on the a2-g8 diagonal comes to an unfortunate end. The lesser evil is 23...♗d7 24 ♖ac1 (24 ♗c4 ♔g7 25 ♖d4 etc.) 24...♗c6 25 ♗c4 with a clear advantage to White according to Kasparov.

The prospect of ♗c4(+) is decisive, e.g. 25...♗h6 26 ♗c4!, while 25...d5 26 ♗f3 will soon decide.

Despite having no definite order or form, White's initiative seemed to quite naturally take on near decisive proportions without having to resort to anything out of the ordinary. Yet again the gambit pawns were not missed, rather championed by the cause in the form of White's seemingly ceaseless pressure.

From Kasparov we turn to a favourite from an earlier generation – Boris Spassky, who also deservedly features a few times in these pages.

Spassky-Petrosian
World Championship 1969

1 e4 c5 2 ♘f3 d6 3 d4 cxd4 4 ♘xd4 ♘f6 5 ♘c3 a6 6 ♗g5 ♘bd7 7 ♗c4 ♛a5 8 ♛d2 h6 9 ♗xf6 ♘xf6 10 0-0-0 e6 11 ♖he1

You either do or don't like this kind of position. Both sides can expect to be the subject of an attack against the king at some point, with Black's apparent delay in development often rather deceptive.

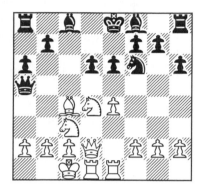

11...⌂e7?

Cafferty gives 11...⌂d7 12 f4 0-0-0 which, while not too common in the main line of the Sicilian (opposite sides castling in the complex lines is what attracts most players), is the best policy here. Then both 13 e5 and 13 f5 can be met with 13...d5.

12 f4

White is happy for Black to castle kingside because he plans to launch an attack there, and the standard 12 ⌂b1 might induce Black to look for alternatives in view of 12...0-0?! 13 ⌂d5 etc.

12...0-0 13 ⌂b3 ⌂e8 14 ⌂b1 ⌂f8 15 g4!

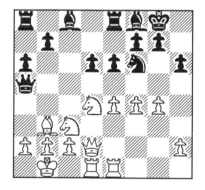

A typical gambit in this kind of situa-

tion, where time, open lines and the initiative are inter-related and incredibly important. Failure to give these factors the respect they deserve can be disastrous, so it is vital to try and get in the first blow. Spassky's gambit offer here is particularly effective because the thrust of the g-pawn in itself is sufficiently threatening to cause the opposition problems if the offer is refused. For example if Black reacts in Sicilian style by ignoring the advance and setting his own in motion on the queenside with 15...b5, then 16 g5 hxg5 17 fxg5 ⌂h5 18 g6! steps up the pace and leaves White in the driving seat after 18...fxg6 19 ⌕g5

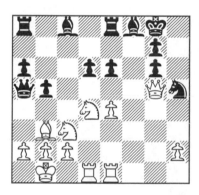

If you play such openings it is imperative that you are constantly on the lookout for disruptive sacrifices such as g5-g6 here, where White is able to assume the initiative without delay and give his opponent defensive worries about the light squares in front of the king, the open files and the a2-g8 diagonal.

The role of pawns in an initiative-driven strategy tends to differ from the norm quite dramatically in that the way a pawn leaves the arena can be crucial.

The rewards of putting the opposition under pressure are juicy enough to reassess how we use pawns, making long-term, structurally oriented measures practically redundant in certain scenarios.

15...♘xg4

White also had to consider a response in the centre, namely 15...e5. Then 16 fxe5 appears easier for White after either 16...dxe5 17 ♘f5 ♗xf5 18 gxf5 ♖ad8 19 ♕g2, when the bishop homes in on f7, or 16...♕xe5 17 ♘f3 followed by g4-g5 etc.

With these possibilities in mind Black elects to accept the gambit and soak up some pressure on the kingside, with the hope of later generating counterplay or simply holding on to emerge with a material lead.

16 ♕g2 ♘f6

16...e5 17 ♘f5 doesn't help Black.

17 ♖g1

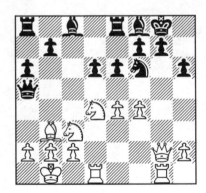

An obvious relocation. For the gambit pawn White has gained time, space and, consequently, a head start in the attacking stakes. White should be happy to part with a pawn if this means earning a place in the driver's seat, and the new, tense situation introduces both f4-f5 and e4-e5 as ways of injecting more venom into the initiative. Meanwhile, White should not have to worry too much about the safety of his own king.

17...♗d7

17...♕c5 18 ♘f3 ♗d7 19 e5! favours White.

18 f5! ♔h8

Black might be able to get away with the positionally suspect 18...e5, accentuating the scope of White's bishop but keeping the centre more closed than in the game.

19 ♖df1

The second rook finds a more promising home, White's latest perhaps serving to intimidate Black merely by placing the rook on the same file as the now unprotected f7-pawn.

19...♕d8

Black does not want to open the a2-f7 diagonal. In response to Geller's suggestion of 19...e5 Cafferty gives 20 ♘e6 fxe6 21 fxe6 ♗xe6 22 ♖xf6 but misses 21...♖xe6!, which is good for Black. Consequently the best move is 20 ♘de2.

Returning to the text, the retreat of the queen is indicative of the success thus far of White's gambit. Downscaling the queen's role from that of a potential attack leader to defender is tantamount to acknowledging White's initiative.

20 fxe6

As for White, he is intent on opening lines in order to cause maximum inconvenience.

20...fxe6

A difficult choice as Black is understandably reluctant to part with his light-squared bishop even if this removes a pair of minor pieces: 20...♗xe6 21 ♘xe6 fxe6 22 ♘e2 and the threat to hit the weak light squares with ♘f4 forces 22...e5, when 23 ♗f7 ♖e7 walks into 24 ♖xf6! etc.

21 e5!

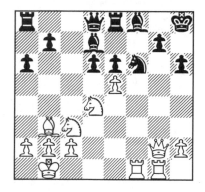

Clearing the way for the hitherto quiet c3-knight to jump into action. White has a number of pieces in attacking positions and plans to remove the key defender on f6. 21 ♘f3 followed by ♘h4 or e4-e5 is another possibility.

21...dxe5 22 ♘e4!?

Black is passive and struggling. White's initiative is such that he can play aggressive moves with confidence, needing to be careful (we should always be careful!) only in terms of miscalculation. Now that the roles of the players have been clearly defined the sense of urgency is less evident, for White is no longer likely to come under attack himself and can therefore approach his own offensive with a touch more patience. Incidentally, do we even notice that White is two pawns down at the moment? Hardly.

22...♘h5

22...exd4 23 ♘xf6 is out of the question, and 22...♘xe4? 23 ♖xf8+ leads to

immediate mate on g7.

23 ♕g6

White cannot be held at bay.

23...exd4

23...♘f4 24 ♖xf4! exf4 25 ♘f3 will net White a king or queen, e.g. 25...♗c6 26 ♘eg5 hxg5 27 ♘xg5, when 27...♕xg5 28 ♖xg5 ♗f3 (28...♗d5 29 ♖xd5 exd5 30 ♕h5+ ♔g8 31 ♗xd5+) 29 ♗xe6 ♖xe6 30 ♕xe6 (threatening ♕h3+ and ♕xf3) 30...♗d1 31 ♖d5 is an instructive finish.

24 ♘g5! 1-0

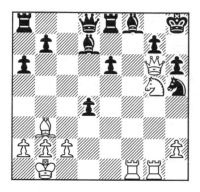

Black resigned rather than play out the finish 24...hxg5 25 ♕xh5+ ♔g8 26 ♕f7+ ♔h8 27 ♖f3 etc.

Incidentally, I write these words after seeing on television a documentary that featured quite non-standard chess sets. In reply to the question as to how he would cope playing with some of the more unusual sets, GM Jonathan Levitt replied that GMs don't really need a set to play a game. The following example, in fact, was played under such blindfold conditions. White's handling of the initiative generated by his gambit is both instructive and impressive. Just out of interest, imagine, as the game progresses, how you would manage without a board.

Kramnik-Topalov
Monaco (Blindfold) 1998

1 ♘f3 g6 2 d4 d6 3 c4 ♗g7 4 ♘c3 e5!?

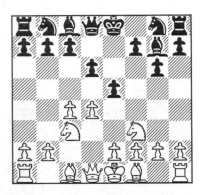

Inviting an exchange of queens to — hopefully — reduce the likelihood of coming under too much pressure against the mighty Kramnik...

5 dxe5 dxe5 6 ♕xd8+ ♔xd8 7 ♗d2 ♗e6 8 0-0-0 ♘d7

Even mere mortals might be able to notice without the aid of a board that 8...♗xc4? 9 ♗g5+ sees mate on d8 next move. If you considered only 9 ♗h6+ followed by ♗xg7 (and ♗xh8) I guess you deserve a light pat on the back. Instead Black develops a piece while ruling out the discovered check.

The other way to do this is with 8...♔c8, when 9 ♘g5 ♗xc4 10 b3 ♗e6 11 ♘xe6 fxe6 12 g3 gives White ample compensation. With the only light-squared bishop, easy targets in e6 and e5 and a potential outpost on e4, this is easy to appreciate.

9 ♘g5

White could defend the c4-pawn but this costs a tempo in a position that won't take too much repairing for Black. Kramnik's choice puts immediate pressure on Black at the cost of a pawn, exploiting the inconvenienced king to generate a long-term initiative.

9...♗xc4

10 e4!?

An interesting departure from 10 b3 ♗e6 11 ♘xe6+ fxe6 12 g3 (Kasparov), which also looks quite pleasant for White. But this time Black need not accept doubled, isolated e-pawns.

10...♗xf1 11 ♖hxf1 ♘h6

Black misplaces his knight as 11...♔e8 runs into 12 ♘b5 etc.

12 f4

The point. The absence of queens might give the impression that aggressive play is not worth striving for, but there are more than enough pieces on the board to make life interesting. By inviting ...♗xf1 White has, by the recapture, brought his rook to a potentially fruitful file and, with Black's f7-pawn already a problem for the defender, this pawn break is perfectly natural.

12...c6 13 fxe5

13 f5 followed by h2-h3, g2-g4 and so on brings about a different game. White's strategy, however, is based on exploiting the weaknesses in the enemy camp in order to maintain a nagging pull. This policy is facilitated by keeping lines open, thus providing better access for White's forces.

13...♔e7

There was also another crafty justification of 13 fxe5, namely 13...♘xe5? 14 ♘e6+, when 14...fxe6 15 ♗xh6+ cleans up. Of course super-GMs should not fall into this even under these circumstances, but who knows?

14 ♘f3

Threatening the check on g5.

**14...♘g4 15 ♗g5+ ♔e8 16 e6!
fxe6 17 ♖d6**

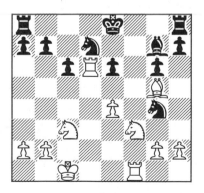

White can try to make something of his initiative only by coming up with a second gambit. This time the aim is to infiltrate further and trouble Black's king – hence the passive reply.

17...♘f8 18 ♖fd1 ♗f6!

18...h6 is an automatic 'chase the unwelcome piece away' response which is a bad habit among club players but hardly seen in top level competition. After 19 ♖d8+ ♖xd8 20 ♖xd8+ ♔f7 21 ♗d2 followed by 22 ♖b8 Black's queenside is conspicuously absent of help. Topalov's move is more logical.

19 e5!?

Another nice try, playing to his strengths in the centre. After 19 ♗xf6 ♘xf6 20 e5 the knight comes to d5.

19...♗xg5+ 20 ♘xg5 ♘xe5

In the event of 20...♘e3 White can contemplate the exchange sacrifice that follows 21 ♖d3 ♘c4 22 ♘ce4, e.g. 22...♘xd6 23 ♘xd6+ ♔e7 24 ♖f3

Black's rooks are no match for the enemy knights here and, despite the fact that White is an exchange and a pawn down in the diagram position, his chances are preferable. An amusing finish here would be 24...♘d7?? 25 ♖f7+ ♔d8 26 ♘xe6 mate. After 24...h6 25

♖f7+ ♚d8 26 ♘xb7+ ♚e8 27 ♘d6+ ♚d8 White certainly has better than to take the draw, e.g. 28 ♘ge4 ♘d7 29 ♘b7+ ♚c8 30 ♘ed6+ ♚c7 31 ♘c5 etc. Finally, something like 24...b5 permits 25 ♖f7+ ♚d8 26 ♖g7! and the fork on f7 is coming. I must say that, although I didn't use Fritz to find these last couple of variations, nor was I blindfold, either.

21 ♘xe6 ♚e7 22 ♘d8!?

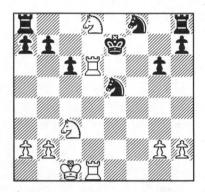

White's initiative is probably not as powerful as it first appears, but the onus is on Black to continue to defend accurately. Should White restore material equilibrium his other advantages will remain intact.

22...♖b8

Not 22...♘f7? 23 ♖e1+! ♚xd6 24 ♘xf7+ etc. Black simply holds on.

23 ♘e4 ♘fd7

Missing 23...♘c4! 24 ♖xc6 ♖xd8 25 ♖xc4 with a draw on the cards.

24 ♖e6+ ♚xd8

Black is struggling after 24...♚f8 25 ♖f1+ ♚g7 26 ♖e7+ ♚h6 27 ♘f7+ ♘xf7 28 ♖fxf7.

25 ♖xe5 ♖f8?!

Again Black had a better option in the entertaining variation 25...♖e8 26 ♘f6!? (26 ♖xd7+ ♚xd7 27 ♘f6+ ♚d6

28 ♖xe8 ♖xe8 29 ♘xe8+ ♚e7 and the knight is trapped) 26...♖xe5 27 ♘xd7

Imagine having to work this out blindfold. Topalov can be forgiven for failing to latch on to the most appropriate course. Here after 27...♖d5 28 ♘xb8 ♚c7 29 ♘xc6 it is time to split the point.

26 ♘c5 ♖f7 27 ♖e3! b6?

Another natural move under the circumstances. There was an odd draw in 27...♚c7 28 ♘e6+ ♚b6 (28...♚c8 29 ♘g5, and 29...♖g7?? loses to 30 ♖e8+ ♚c7 31 ♘e6+) 29 ♖b3+ ♚a5 30 ♖a3+ when White has nothing better than to keep checking. Kramnik now produces an unexpected resource that sees White emerge with an extra piece.

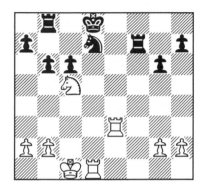

28 ♖f3! ♖xf3

It is worth noting how the unfortunately placed king has contributed to White's being able – with a little help from Topalov – to keep the initiative alive. Now 28...♖e7 29 ♘xd7 ♖xd7 30 ♖f8+ ♔c7 31 ♖xd7+ will leave Black a rook down.

29 ♘xd7

A very nice attractive way to conclude the game. White's knight now manages to hop to safety.

29...♖f2 30 ♘xb8+ ♔c7 31 ♘a6+ ♔b7

Or 31...♔c8 32 ♖d2! ♖xd2 33 ♔xd2 c5 34 b4 ♔b7 35 b5 etc.

32 ♘b4 c5 33 ♘c2 ♔c6

33...♖xg2 34 ♖d7+.

34 ♖d2 ♖f1+ 35 ♖d1 ♖f2 36 ♖g1 g5 37 h3 h5 38 ♘e1 c4 39 ♘f3 c3 40 bxc3 ♖xa2 41 ♔b1 ♖f2 42 ♘xg5 ♔d5 43 g4 h4 44 ♖d1+ ♔c4 45 ♘e4 ♖h2 46 g5 ♔b3 47 ♖g1 a5 48 g6 1-0

CHAPTER FOUR

Outposts

We often hear the advice that a 'rook on the seventh rank is the equivalent of being a pawn up' but an effective outpost is at least as important. A gambit designed mainly to transfer a piece to an influential, safe square can help mould the shape of the game in the aggressor's favour.

Kramnik-Gelfand
Novgorod 1996

1 ♘f3 ♘f6 2 c4 g6 3 ♘c3 ♗g7 4 e4 d6 5 d4 0-0 6 ♗e2 e5 7 0-0 ♘c6 8 d5 ♘e7

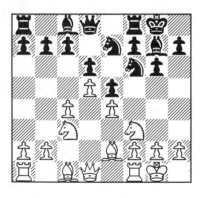

This starting position of main line of

the King's Indian Defence has been seen countless times at all levels. Expanding in the centre with d4-d5 sends the attacked knight to join its partner on the kingside, where Black tends to put his hopes in a vicious attack against the king, unleashing the f-pawn, often the g-pawn, an army of pieces and – if need be – the kitchen sink! White's space advantage is on the other flank, which is where his (counter-)play takes place, typically spearheaded by b2-b4, c4-c5 etc. Obviously the nature of the struggle in this line is not to everyone's taste, and Black's potentially devastating attacks can be incredibly intimidating to face even when they don't work! In this game Kramnik opts to quickly set his queenside offensive in motion, keeping the momentum going with a gambit that secures excellent outposts for his knights in the centre.

9 b4

One of a number of options, the text wastes no time. White adds to his presence on the queenside and supports a subsequent c4-c5. As for Black, he continues with the mission...

9...♘h5 10 ♖e1 f5 11 c5

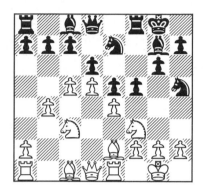

11...fxe4

A new move at the time. Black wants to put immediate use to his influence on the f-file and f4-square in particular. Before this encounter Black had returned the knight with 11...♘f6 or invested a tempo on 11...♔h8, tucking the king away and leaving the g8-square available for a knight or a rook. While the text does open lines for Black (as well as the f-file, the light-squared bishop now has a clear view of the enemy kingside), the price is White's new and potentially promising outpost on e4.

12 ♘xe4 ♘f4 13 ♗xf4

The unwelcome knight cannot be allowed to remain on f4, so it is a question here of what White intends to do about the stand-off involving c5 and d6. Kramnik suggests inserting 13 cxd6!? cxd6 before the capture on f4 in order to fix the centre pawns after 14 ♗xf4 ♖xf4 15 ♘fd2.

13...♖xf4 14 ♘fd2!?

White plans, quite simply, to relieve the d2-knight of its defensive duties and leave it free to come to c4, from where d6 can be attacked.

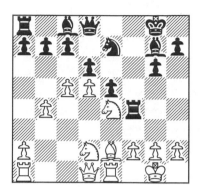

14...dxc5!

Black grasps the nettle and admits that the middlegame will focus on the middle of the playing area. Rather than see a d6-pawn come under fire, Gelfand prefers to soak up a little pressure. While such decisions are often partly influenced by our style of play and psychological make-up, it is not unusual to have to go along with the opponent's plans occasionally, collecting the gift and allowing the opposition the compensation (as long as this does not far outweigh the initial price of the gambit).

15 ♗c4 ♘xd5

15...♔h8 16 ♘xc5 ♘xd5 17 ♘de4 is the same as the game after 17...c6.

16 ♘b3 c6 17 ♘bxc5

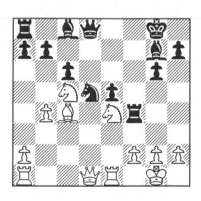

No doubt both players had the diagram position in mind a few moves earlier. In the space of just a few moves White has (voluntarily) seen the disappearance of his three centre pawns! So what does White have for the pawn deficit? Well, his remaining minor pieces all occupy excellent outposts right in the heart of the arena, thus affording him considerable influence across the board. The c5-knight hinders Black's development by keeping the b7-pawn in its sights, the bishop pins Black's only active-looking minor piece and the other knight reigns supreme on e4, majestically posted directly in front of an isolated pawn (traditionally the ideal location for a knight). Meanwhile White enjoys freedom for his major pieces, a safe king position and two pawn islands to Black's three. This latter positional plus is, of course, because Black has an extra pawn(!) which, along with the soon to be unpinned knight and the odd-looking but nonetheless would-be threatening rook, is what Black is pinning is hopes on. White's compensation is obvious, and Black is sufficiently solid to hold the balance with accurate play. This is a rather modern, high level gambit situation in which the investment offers decent practical chances but the 'defender' is confident enough in his abilities to keep his head above water.

17...♔h8

Kramnik gives 17...b5? 18 ♗xb5! cxb5 19 ♕b3 with a clear advantage to White. The point behind ...b7-b5 is to bother the pinning bishop and prevent the undermining of the defence of the knight on d5 with b4-b5, but the sacrifice has left White's pin even more annoying. The displacement of the c6-pawn puts extra pressure on the knight, which will be in trouble on the d-file even after the original pin is lifted with ...♔h8. Here 19...♗g4 20 f3 leaves White on top.

We must also consider 17...b6?, hoping to evict White's other well placed and most advanced piece. However, after 18 ♕a4! b5 19 ♗xb5 cxb5 20 ♕b3 we are back in the 17...b5 line, while 18...♕c7 19 ♗xd5+ cxd5 20 ♕b3 is clearly better for White according to Kramnik.

With the sensible text Black refuses to be drawn into reacting to the enemy pieces and their impressive new homes. Instead Gelfand simply steps out of the pin and waits to see how White tries to justify his gambit.

18 b5

The centre pawns have gone but the b-pawn remains, so White adds to the pressure by concentrating on the c6-pawn (and in turn the d5-knight). Remember that knights in particular are optimally posted directly in front of isolated pawns, so the trade on c6 (b5xc6 b7xc6) would rule out a future ...b7-b6 and leave the knight sitting pretty on c5. 18 ♕d2 looks sensible but is less immediate and presents Black with an opportunity to mix things with 18...♗f5!, e.g. 19 g3 ♗xe4 20 gxf4 ♗f3, when White suddenly has concerns on the kingside, or 20 ♘xe4 ♖f8 with one less active minor piece for White and a slightly damaged defensive wall in front of his king.

18...♖f8

The rook returns to the fold, also

providing the knight with an outpost on f4, perhaps.

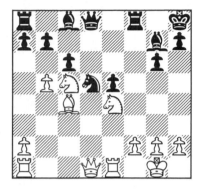

19 ℤb1

Another point of the previous retreat of the rook is that the active 19 ℤc1 (with a view to attacking what might soon be an isolated pawn on c6, and supporting the knight) can be met with 19...♗h6. Finding the best file for a rook can be a difficult task even for the strongest players, so another option here is 19 ♛b3!?, keeping the queen in touch with matters on the queenside and adding a third possible home for the queen's rook in d1. Then Kramnik gives 19...♘b6 20 bxc6 bxc6 21 ♗e6

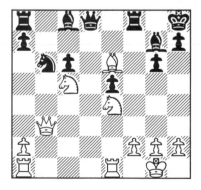

White certainly has compensation for the gambit pawn here. As we can see from the examples in this chapter, the gambit of a pawn or more for an excellent outpost can have quite different results. In this case both white knights occupy squares in front of isolated pawns and, while White is reasonably actively placed, the flavour of the compensation is essentially positional. Even if White cannot find a way in the onus is still on Black to deal with the almost untouchable knights.

19...♘b6?!

Kramnik prefers keeping the queens on with 19...♛c7!, when he evaluates the position after 20 bxc6 bxc6 as unclear. This is perfectly reasonable, and the matter of the side of the board on which you feel more comfortable comes down to individual style and taste and so on. Concentrating only on the pieces and their location points undoubtedly to pleasant prospects for White, who should not be at all concerned with the fact that he is a pawn down. Black, on the other hand, is well aware of his slight material lead and, for his part, should exploit this factor to keep White on his toes and perhaps steer the game into territory where exchanges play a leading role.

There is also the prospect of advantageously returning material to consider, and here you might have noticed the following variation: 21 ♗xd5 ℤd8 22 ♗xc6 (22 ♗e6!? ℤxd1 23 ℤexd1 is another possibility but Kramnik's suggestion 23...♗f8! might relieve some of the pressure) 22...ℤxd1 23 ℤexd1 ♛xc6 24 ℤd8+ ♗f8 25 ℤxf8+ ♚g7 26 ℤd8

See following diagram

A slight material imbalance has resulted from the multiple trades, but the knights still occupy their perfect posts!

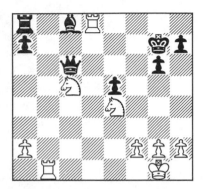

That this feature remains intact so long after the initial gambit (of which the knights were the main intended beneficiaries) is a testament to the soundness of White's idea. Meanwhile, despite having reached move 26, Black is yet to actually pick up his remaining rook and bishop. Of course White is not compelled to sacrifice the queen, but the very 'points' nature of gambits – even the modern positional variety – tends to require both sides to loosen up and to be prepared for less usual situations. After the text White is invited to turn his attentions to the kingside.

20 ♕xd8 ♖xd8

21 ♘g5

Alternatively White can first tidy up on the other flank: 21 bxc6 bxc6 22 ♘g5 ♖f8! and now instead of the hasty 23 ♘f7+ ♔g8 24 ♘xe5+ ♘xc4 25 ♘xc4 ♗d4, when the bishops threaten to make their presence felt, the calm 23 ♗b3 is interesting after 23...h6 24 ♘f7+ ♔h7 25 ♘xe5 ♗f5 26 ♖bc1 ♖ae8 27 f4

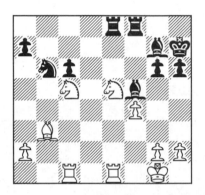

Note that 27 ♘xc6? runs into 27...♖xe1+ 28 ♖xe1 ♖c8 but now after the thematic 27...g5 White can grab the pawn: 28 ♘xc6 ♖xe1+ (28...gxf4 29 ♘e6 is very nice for White) 29 ♖xe1 ♖c8 30 ♗e6 ♗xe6 31 ♖xe6 gxf4 32 ♘d3 with a definite pull in the ending.

21...♖d4

21...♖f8!? 22 ♗b3 h6 23 ♘f7+ ♔h7 24 bxc6 bxc6 25 ♘xe5 transposes to the previous note.

22 ♗b3 cxb5 23 ♘f7+

Better than 23 ♖bd1 ♖xd1 24 ♖xd1 ♗f6.

23...♔g8 24 ♘d6+

More troublesome for Black than 24 ♘xe5+ ♘c4 25 a4 a6 etc.

24...♔h8 25 ♘f7+ ♔g8 26 ♘d6+ ♔h8 27 ♘xb5!

No draw (yet). White's initial gambit was designed to give his knights an opportunity to shine, and there is no reason to share the point while both pieces continue to enjoy such freedom and activity, particularly when Black is without any counterplay.

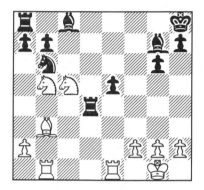

27...♖d8 28 ♖bd1

Contesting the d-file and challenging Black's only good looking piece.

28...♖xd1 29 ♖xd1 ♗f6 30 ♘d6 ♗e7

Part of Black's defensive strategy has been to go along for the ride, soak up the pressure and be willing to return the pawn at an opportune moment. But how will White react?

31 ♘cxb7?!

By now we have passed the 30th move and White's army is much smaller than when he initiated the gambit. In such situations, still a pawn down and with ostensibly fewer possibilities to actually make something of the gambit, it is very easy indeed – even for the top players – to finally cash in on the investment and restore material equilibrium. The net result when the defender has been managing to holding his game together tends to be approximate equality. However, White's knights continue to dominate proceedings and his other two 'play' pieces could hardly be better placed, so White would be justified in sitting on the position and maintaining the pressure with a useful move such as 31 h3, or increasing it with 31 a4!?, both of which Kramnik prefers. The text eases Black's defensive task, trading a great knight for a bishop that has not even moved thus far(!) and freeing the rook.

31...♗xb7 32 ♘xb7 ♔g7 33 ♔f1 ♖b8 34 ♘d6 ♖d8 35 ♘b5 ♖xd1+ 36 ♗xd1

It seems that White has settled for splitting the point. The isolated e5-pawn is Black's only concern, but a draw is on the cards. The game continued:

36...a6 37 ♘a7 ♘d5 38 ♘c6 ♗d6

39 ♗e2 ♘b4!

Exploiting the fact that the bishops operate on different colour squares.

40 ♘xb4 ♗xb4 41 ♗xa6 ♔f6 42 ♗b7 ♔f5 43 f3 h5!

Many players would make the mistake of automatically placing their pawns on dark squares, but Kramnik points out that 43...h6 44 ♔e2 g5? 45 ♗e4+ ♔e6 46 g4! leaves White with a clear advantage.

44 ♗c8+

44 h4 g5 is equal.

44...♔f6 45 a4 h4 46 ♔e2 ♔e7 47 ♔d3 ♔d6 48 ♗b7 ♗a5 49 ♗e4 g5

Note that Black's pawn is better on h4 than fixed on h6.

50 ♔c4 ♗b6 51 ♔b5 ♔c7 ½-½

In our next example Kramnik again finds a way to establish a knight in the middle of the board, but this time his sights are more specifically set on the enemy kingside ...

Kramnik-Malaniuk
Moscow Olympiad 1994

1 ♘f3 f5

The Dutch Defence tends to be favoured by uncompromising, aggressive players to whom the traditional rule of not moving the f-pawn unless absolutely necessary means nothing. In fact White can try to punish Black's cheeky thrust immediately with 2 e4, when Black has to be careful. However, such an approach is not to everyone's taste, particularly at the top level, so Kramnik prefers to keep his powder dry until a less risky opportunity presents itself, opting instead to adopt an appropriate

set-up that is best suited to the coming pawn structure. (Because Malaniuk is a Leningrad Dutch specialist Kramnik will have had the luxury of at least being able to prepare to some degree for the opening phase of the game.)

2 g3 ♘f6 3 ♗g2 g6 4 0-0 ♗g7 5 d4 d6 6 c4 0-0 7 ♘c3 ♕e8

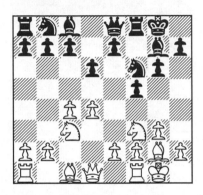

We don't want to worry about opening theory here, suffice to say that from e8 the queen supports the central push with ...e7-e5 and toys with the prospect of swinging over to the kingside after ...h7-h6 and ...g6-g5 etc. Meanwhile the abandoned c7-pawn/square can be protected by ...♘a6.

8 d5

Typical expansion in the centre. Now that the d4-square is vacant the knight can come to the middle of the board to double the attention on the potentially weak e6-square (this 'hole' is a natural drawback of this variation for Black) and team up with the d5-pawn and the g2-bishop (which will enjoy considerable freedom should ...e7-e6/e5 be answered by d5xe6) to clamp down on the c6-point.

8...♘a6 9 ♖b1 ♗d7 10 b4 c5 11 dxc6 ♗xc6

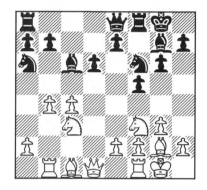

Since the opening move, when Black put in a bid for the e4-square, White has been planning (anticipating this line) to drum up some kind of activity on the queenside – hence the thrust of the b-pawn. Note that after 13 b5 and the trade on f3 Black has 14...♘c5, when the 'dim' knight is transformed into an excellent piece, blockading a backward pawn and adding further weight to Black's grip on e4. In fact in the diagram position Black now has a bishop, knight and pawn all covering this piece of enemy territory. For most players the occupation of e4 might be a cause for concern, but Kramnik has in mind a surprisingly effective gambit aimed at exploiting Black's kingside structure.

12 ♕b3 ♘e4 13 ♗b2 ♘xc3

In hindsight if Black wants a double exchange on c3 he should start with the less natural 13...♗xc3!, when after 14 ♗xc3 ♘xc3 15 ♕xc3 ♖c8 White is slightly better according to Kramnik. The text is theory but walks into an interesting new idea.

14 ♗xc3 ♗xc3 15 c5+!?

Very briefly entertaining this possibility is not the same as evaluating its implications, and this is the kind of move

that can decide the course of a game. White's play thus far has been concentrated on the queenside but the text addresses the new situation on the other flank – namely the disappearance of both black minor pieces. Suddenly Black's kingside structure looks rather awkward, with h6, e6 and g5 being potential troublespots for Black. Meanwhile the advance of the c-pawn is also directed against Black's kingside – as we are about to see.

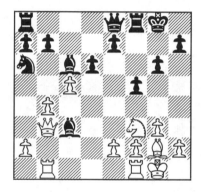

15...e6

In the event of 15...♕f7?! 16 ♕xc3 ♕xa2 Black suffers the traditional punishment for accepting an offer of a distant queenside pawn with his queen: 17 cxd6 exd6 18 ♖a1! and the queen must be careful, for example 18...♕xe2 19 ♘d4 and 18...♕e6 19 ♘d4 lose material, and 18...♕d5 19 ♖a5 should be avoided. Instead the full retreat 18...♕f7 is necessary, when 19 ♘g5! ♕e7 (Kramnik) gives White a clear advantage. Blocking the check with the e-pawn also seems to considerably favour White, but only after accurate, energetic play from the future world champion.

16 ♕xc3 dxc5

Unfortunately for Black 16...♗e4 17

cxd6! &xb1 18 &xb1 works against him because for the exchange White has a passed pawn on the sixth rank, active pieces (the knight is coming to e5 and the bishop has no match) and no genuine weaknesses, whereas Black's major pieces will struggle to get into the game, his knight is awful and the structure susceptible to attack. Alternatively, 16...&xf3 17 &xf3 d5 hopes to close out the bishop with a (rigid) wall of pawns, but this effectively gives White a 3-2 pawn majority on the queenside, which can be put to immediate use with 18 b5, gaining time on the hapless knight in the process.

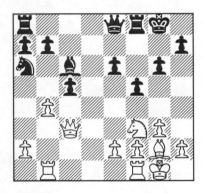

17 b5!

The point. After the automatic 17 bxc5?! &c8 White has the b-file and the e5-square but the isolated c-pawn (and the menacing c8-rook) are more than enough to worry White. Now, for the price of two pawns, White is able to exploit the e5-square and enjoy an initiative without giving Black such easy counterplay.

17...&xb5 18 ♘e5

18 ♘g5 features a more immediate plan of putting Black under pressure on both flanks. Then after 18...&c6! 19

&xb7 &xb7 20 &xb7 Black should play 20...♕e7! 21 &xa8 &xa8 with a pawn to show for his weaknesses and a less powerful army to face, rather than 21...♕xg5 22 &b7 etc.

18...&b8

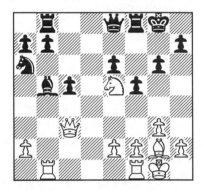

In for a penny, in for a pound as my grandmother might have said. In other words, White's initial gambit holds genuine promise only if a second gambit is made. If White wants maximum value for his outpost he must be prepared to invest accordingly, and it is this willingness to part with more than a single pawn that tends to put most of us off gambit play – if, indeed, we manage to find such possibilities. Gifting the opponent a pawn seems okay, but isn't two rather generous? What if the overall gambit proves to be ill-judged? Well, that's life. Nobody is perfect, and we will make poor decisions, but leaving ourselves open to the gambit style of play – when appropriate – will both enrich our games and improve our results. Anyway, a successful gambit of two pawns will put the opposition under more pressure than a less promising gambit of one.

19 &fe1!

Sensibly protecting the e2-pawn while preparing to accentuate White's influence in the centre by opening the e-file with e2-e4 etc. There was another option in 19 g4, when after 19...♗xe2 20 ♖fe1 ♗xg4 21 ♖xb7 ♖xb7 22 ♗xb7 careful defence is required from Black.

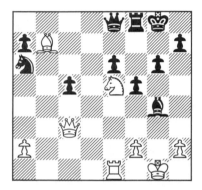

22...♘b8 23 ♘xg4 fxg4 24 ♗d5 exd5 25 ♖xe8 ♖xe8 26 ♕xc5 favours the queen, well placed to operate on both flanks, while 22...♘b4 23 ♕xc5 is clearly better for White according to Kramnik. More complex is 22...♕b5 23 ♗xa6 ♕xa6 24 ♘d7 ♖c8 (24...♖d8!? – Kramnik) 25 ♘f6+ (25 ♕f6 ♕d6) 25...♔f7 26 ♘xh7, when White is still two pawns down but Black has major problems on the dark squares. Best seems 22...♘c7! 23 ♕xc5 ♕d8 with a more compact position for Black. The onus certainly seems on White to demonstrate genuine compensation here.

Meanwhile, 19 ♕a5 ♗xe2 20 ♖fe1 b6! is simply too much for White to donate after 21 ♕a3 ♗b5. Despite what I said in the note to Black's 18th move, we must draw the line somewhere unless the situation dictates a further gambit (or gambits). Each offer must be accompanied with a realistic aim or plan.

Returning to the position after 19 ♖fe1, Black would like to withdraw his pawns to g7 and f7 in order to avoid an offensive from White in this sector, where his knight is almost single-handedly overseeing proceedings. Over on the queenside Black has a 3–1 pawn majority, but this advantage might take a long time to come into play (if at all).

19...b6

Consolidating, although this does leave the c6-square vulnerable. Note that White's knight is causing problems for Black on both wings. Kramnik gives 19...♗c6, when White is able to profit from his superior minor pieces by parting with the one for which the gambit was originally designed. After 20 ♘xc6 bxc6 21 ♕a5 Black's scattered pawns present White with a favourable cashback opportunity, e.g. 21...♖xb1 22 ♖xb1 ♕c8 23 e3 followed by ♗f1, when the extra pawns are doubled and isolated and the difference in the bishop and knight is plain to see. This leaves 21...♘b4 22 ♕xc5 ♘d5 (22...♘xa2? runs into 23 ♕c4, and 22...♖b5 23 ♕xa7 ♖f7 24 ♕a4 is uncomfortable for Black) 23 ♖xb8 ♕xb8 24 ♕xc6

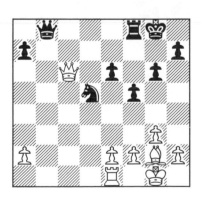

Here we have a situation typical of positionally aggressive gambit play. Having invested two pawns for a great outpost and the pull that accompanies it, White now finds himself level on points but leading in other aspects, namely a long-range bishop (versus a troubled knight), active queen and the superior pawn structure. Black's Achilles heel here is the e6-pawn, which might come under more fire after the thematic e2-e4 etc. Can we blame Black's choice of the Dutch Defence for such a predicament? Perhaps that would be too critical (I've always had the urge to include the Dutch in my repertoire...), but after 1...f5 Black can't exactly complain about holes in his kingside structure as the game gets busy (... I've always been wary of playing the Dutch).

20 e4

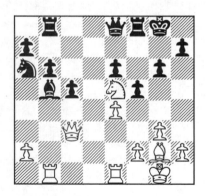

White's game is considerably easier to conduct than his opponent's. Black's king is not in immediate danger but his kingside is beginning to creak, the pawns already committed to unfavourable posts and the queen – currently protecting the bishop – sharing the same file as White's rook. The squares e5, e6, f6, h6, c6, d6 and d7 are all potential trouble spots for Black, whose knight has been conspicuously out of action since the 8th move, a point which needs addressing now if Black is to either bolster the defence of his kingside or distract White from it.

20...♞c7

Coming to the aid of the liability on e6 is the natural response. Kramnik prefers the more active 20...♞b4! with a number of detailed variations. The first point to note is that Black is holding after 21 a3 ♞c6! 22 ♖xb5 ♞xe5 23 ♕xe5 ♕xb5 24 ♕xe6+ ♖f7 25 exf5 ♕d7. This leaves 21 exf5 gxf5 22 a3 and now 22...♞c6 is quite different: 23 ♖xb5! ♞xe5 24 ♕xe5 ♕xb5 25 ♕xe6+ ♖f7 (25...♔g7 26 ♕e5+ ♔h6 27 ♕d6+ is decisive) 26 ♗d5 ♖bf8 27 ♕xf5 and White will emerge on top. Best is 22...♞d5

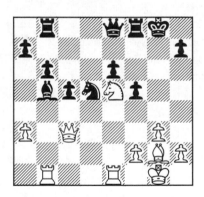

Now White has a few possibilities.

23 ♗xd5 exd5 24 ♕d2 ♗c6! is evaluated as unclear by Kramnik, who continues with the sample line 25 ♕g5+ ♔h8 26 ♕h6 (26 ♞d7 ♗xd7 27 ♖xe8 ♖bxe8) 26...♗a8 27 h4 d4 28 h5 ♗e4, which looks good for Black to me as 29 ♞g6+ ♔g8 30 ♞xf8 ♕xf8 leaves a great

bishop and a wall of pawns.

23 ♕b3 ♗a4 (23...♗c6? 24 ♘xc6 ♕xc6 25 ♖xe6!) 24 ♕c4 ♖d8 25 ♘f3!? maintains some pressure for the two pawns, although Black's prospects appear to be improving.

23 ♕b2!? is another suggestion of Kramnik, but his favourite here is 23 ♕d2, e.g. 23...♘f6 24 ♕g5+ (24 ♖bd1!?) 24...♔h8 25 ♕h6 ♗a4 (25...♗a6 26 ♖bd1) 26 ♖bc1!? (followed by ♖c4-h4) 26...♕h5 (26...♘g8!?) 27 ♕f4 with an interesting struggle ahead.

21 exf5 gxf5

21...♖xf5 invites 22 ♗h3! ♖h5 (22...♘d5 23 ♕b2; 22...♖f8 23 ♘g4) 23 ♘g4!

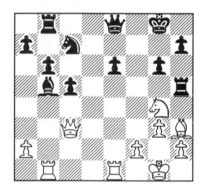

This is the kind of position we try to avoid after accepting a gambit. Suddenly Black's extra pawns and pieces on the queenside don't seem very relevant, while the weaknesses on the kingside do. Then after 23...♘d5 24 ♘f6+ ♘xf6 White throws in 25 ♗xe6+! ♔g7 and can follow up with the discovered attack 26 ♗g4, when 26...♕c6 27 ♖e7+ and 28 ♖e6 (or the immediate 27 ♖e6) should favour White.

22 ♕e3

Bringing the queen within striking distance of Black's kingside and consequently upping the tension. Having set his stall out so early in the game White must have been quite content with the diagram position. The knight is firmly established on e5, the e6-pawn needs protection, Black's kingside defences have been seriously damaged, the bishop is under pressure on b5, the c6-square is vulnerable, he is uncomfortably passive...

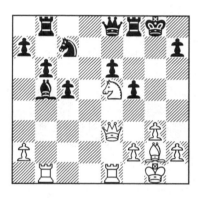

From a practical point of view most of us would tend to prefer sitting on White's side of the board here. In fact his game has been easier to play since the gambit theme was introduced, regardless of Black's defensive resources. What we can see now as we play through the game in – I hope – an atmosphere of comfort and calm (and without a clock eating up valuable thinking time) cannot be compared with Malaniuk's circumstances during the game, especially when we remind ourselves that the mighty Kramnik is in charge of the white pieces. Black's structure from the outset is such that White's gambit approach is guaranteed to have some level of success because certain potentially important squares will inevitably come under pressure, a fact that is rather reassuring for White.

22...a6?!

With his knight tied down to both e6 and b5 and the queen defending e6, b5 and the kingside, Black opts to safeguard the piece that protects c6. This is an important stage of the game, so let us investigate the alternatives:

22...♕e7 covers g5 and connects the rooks but then 23 ♗c6! ♗a6 (23...a6 24 ♗xb5 and 25 ♘c6) 24 ♘d7 cashes in favourably for White.

22...♘d5 23 ♕g5+ ♔h8 works out fine for Black after 24 ♖xb5 ♕xb5 25 ♘g6+ hxg6 26 ♕h6+ ♔g8 27 ♕xg6+ ♔h8, e.g. 28 ♗xd5 28...exd5 29 ♖e7 ♕b1+ 30 ♔g2 ♕e4+ 31 ♖xe4 dxe4 32 ♕h6+ ♔g8 33 ♕g6+, or 28 ♕h6+ ♔g8 29 ♖xe6!? (29 ♕xe6+ ♔g7) 29...♕b1+ 30 ♗f1

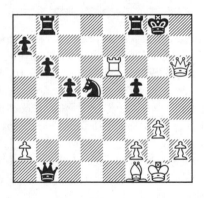

30...♖f6! 31 ♖xf6 ♘xf6 32 ♕g6+ ♔h8 33 ♕xf6+ ♔h7 etc.

However, with 24 ♗xd5 24...exd5 25 ♘f3 White can win material due to the threat of ♖e7, e.g. 25...♕g6 (25...♕c6 26 ♖e7 ♖g8 27 ♕xf5 ♖g7 28 ♖xg7 ♔xg7 29 ♕e5+) 26 ♕xg6 hxg6 27 ♖xb5 and Black has two pawns for a piece as opposed to two extra pawns.

After 22...♖d8 23 ♕g5+ ♔h8 24 ♕h6 (24 ♗f3!? is a suggestion from Kramnik) 24...♖g8 (24...♖d4? 25 ♖xb5!; 24...a6 25 ♗f3) there comes 25 ♖xb5!?

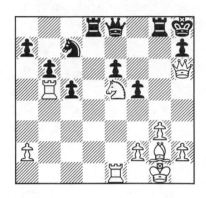

This has been on the cards for a while, the main point being the mate on f7 should Black recapture with the queen. After 25...♘xb5 the contribution of White's super-knight is made on the queenside: 26 ♗c6 ♕f8 27 ♕xf8 ♖gxf8 28 ♗xb5 with a pull thanks to the combined power of the minor pieces.

22...♗a4 removes the bishop from the firing line and monitors d1. Again 23 ♖bc1!? followed by swinging over to h4 via c4 is a possibility, as are 23 ♕f4!? and 23 h4!?, while Kramnik gives 23 ♗f3 ♘d5! (23...♕e7 24 ♗c6) 24 ♕g5+ ♔h8 25 ♕h4!? ♘f6 26 ♖e3!? ♖d8 (26...♗c2 27 ♗c6) 27 ♖be1 ♖d4 28 ♕h6 with threat of ♘g6+.

The common denominator in so many of the variations that we have seen throughout this game is the seemingly effortless fashion in which White is able to pile on the pressure, there being sufficient practical problems for Black to overcome.

23 ♕g5+ ♔h8 24 ♖bd1

White activates the final piece and

addresses a defensive possibility.

24...♖g8

White's previous move set up 24...♘d5 25 ♖xd5! exd5 26 ♗xd5, when 26...♕d8? runs into 27 ♘g6+! ♔g7 (27...hxg6 28 ♕h6 mate) 28 ♖e7+ which should lead to mate in the very near future.

25 ♕f4!

25 ♕f6+ ♖g7 with ...♕e7 to follow gets White nowhere, and 25 ♕h4 ♕f8!? (25...♖g7 26 ♖d6 ♕e7?? 27 ♘g6+ is one to avoid) 26 ♘d7 ♗xd7 27 ♖xd7 ♖g7 28 ♖ed1 ♘d5 holds for Black. The text permits the queen to keep in touch with more than just the kingside.

25...♕e7

25...♖g7 26 ♖d6 ♕e7 (26...♖d8 27

♖xb6) 27 ♖ed1 is Kramnik's suggested lesser evil.

26 ♗c6!

Note the significance of both c6 and d7.

26...♖g4?

An understandable reaction given the amount of pressure Black has had to withstand since Kramnik unleashed the new gambit idea. 26...♖bd8 is necessary, when 27 ♖xd8 ♖xd8 28 ♗xb5 axb5 (28...♖d4 29 ♕h6) 29 ♘c6 ♕d7 30 ♘xd8 ♕xd8 appears favourable for White's major pieces, particularly in view of Black's still vulnerable king.

27 ♘xg4 ♗xc6 28 ♖d6!

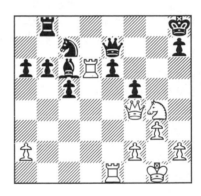

Thanks to his dropping the queen back to f4 White (finally) exploits yet another weak spot in Black's camp.

28...♗e8

28...♗d5 29 ♖xd5.

29 ♘h6?!

Short of time, White misses 29 ♖dxe6! ♘xe6 30 ♕e5+ (or 30 ♕xb8 fxg4 31 ♕e5+) 30...♕g7 (30...♔g8 31 ♘h6+ with mate next move) 31 ♕xb8 etc.

29...♖c8 30 ♖xb6 ♕g7

30...♕f6 31 ♘g4 ♕g7 32 ♘e3.

31 ♖b7 ♗c6 32 ♖a7 ♘d5 33 ♕e5!

Time to trade in one advantage for another.

33...♕xe5 34 ♘f7+! ♔g8 35 ♘xe5

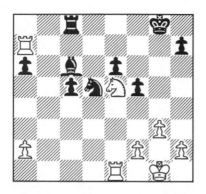

As if by magic, the knight returns to the perfect outpost. Kramnik must have been very pleased to see his gambit 'justified' and the theme maintained twenty moves after it began.

35...♗b5 36 a4!

The bishop has had no peace on the b5-square.

36...♗xa4 37 ♖xa6 ♗b5

37...♗b3 38 ♖xe6.

38 ♖xe6 c4 39 ♖d6 ♘b4 40 ♖b6 ♘c2 41 ♖b1!

1-0

A possible finish is 41...♘a3 (41...♗a4 42 ♖b8) 42 ♖1xb5 ♘xb5 43 ♖xb5 c3 44 ♖b1 etc. An excellent demonstration of the positional, aggressive, long-term gambit.

Accepting gambits can be awkward on a good day, but we are often told that doing so with the queen is particularly risky. Watch how White, sitting on a space advantage and with a super-solid structure, sends his queen down the board to accept what should have been a weak d6-pawn.

Littleton-Boey
Havana Olympiad 1966

1 d4 ♘f6 2 c4 g6 3 ♘c3 ♗g7 4 e4 d6 5 ♘f3 0-0 6 ♗e2 e5 7 0-0 exd4 8 ♘xd4 ♖e8 9 f3

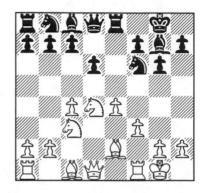

Black has voluntarily surrendered the stronghold on e5 in order to provide his g7-bishop with some breathing space on the long diagonal and give the rook a role on e8. Hitting the e4-pawn has also prompted f2-f3 from White, inviting Black to seek activity on the g1–a7 diagonal.

9...c6

Introducing the possibility of activating the queen on b6 (criss-crossing with the g7-bishop) and giving White something to think about in the centre now that the break with ...d6-d5 is a prospect. White's next both removes the knight from a potentially hazardous post and clamps down on d5.

10 ♘c2 ♗e6 11 ♘e3

White continues to monitor the d5-square, but there is an argument for simply completing development with 11 ♗e3, when ...d6-d5 can perhaps be met with c4xd5 followed by e4-e5 with play against the (isolated) d5-pawn and good use of the square in front of it. Meanwhile White would be ready to bring his queen's rook to d1 and look to exploit his territorial advantage. The effect of the text is to clog up White's forces, leaving the dark-squared bishop without a natural outlet.

11...♘a6

The a6-square tends to be a suitable spot for the knight in a number of King's Indian variations, often en route to c5, after which the new outpost will be secured with ...a7-a5.

12 ♕d2

White would like to complete the Maroczy Bind set-up with the desired b2-b3 but here 12 b3? walks into 12...♘xe4!, unleashing the bishop. Note that such a possibility would be unavailable to Black were the a1-rook protected.

12...♕b6

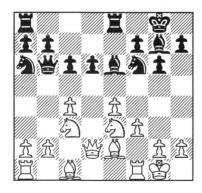

Thanks to White's thematic but rather awkward repositioning of the knight Black has been allowed to mobilise his forces more rapidly, culminating in a pin on the knight and an increased presence on the dark squares (again this would have been ruled out by ♗e3). It is interesting that, regardless of White's

chosen piece configuration, Black would have had the problems that are traditionally associated with the d-pawn when ...e5xd4 has been played. Of course Black tends to generate some form of counterplay in the KID, but his structural shortcomings provide White with long-term grinding out prospects. In the diagram position Black's next will be to actively support the d6-pawn with ...♖ad8, after which White is still required to unravel. Perhaps White did not want to permit this (or was annoyed the possibility itself was of his own making?), or perhaps he had discounted ...♕b6 because it 'loses' a pawn. Whatever the case, he accepts the gambit.

13 ♕xd6?! ♖ad8

The '?!' for ♕xd6 is more a practical criticism. With good play White might well be able to get away with grabbing the pawn but, as is so often the case, finding a safe way back to base and then being able to maintain a clear focus can be a difficult task at the board. A few moves ago Black seemed to be on the way to a fairly cramped, passive middle-game, yet now he has assumed the initiative at the modest cost of a pawn.

14 ♕g3 ♘h5 15 ♕e1

Returning to the fold. Moving any piece too many times during the opening phase is best avoided, and the text is the fourth move of the queen. A more appropriate square might be f2 to break the pin, but ...♗d4 could prove awkward. Also possible is ♕h4, but it is clear that Black has genuine compensation for the gambit pawn in any case.

15...♘f4

Exploiting White's virtual surrender of the dark squares and highlighting one

of the drawbacks of a space advantage –
in this case the potential weaknesses for
White on d4 and d3 that are left behind
by the pawns.

16 ♔h1

It is difficult to see how White can
continue without this unpinning nudge
of the king, although the pressure
mounts after Black's no-nonsense next.
Note that b2-b3 is still out of the question, this time in view of 16 b3?? ♗xc3,
when the recapture loses after ...♘xe2+.

16...♘b4 17 a3

A natural reaction. Fritz suggests 17
♘cd1 ♘fd3 18 ♗xd3 ♘xd3 19 ♕e2
♕c5 20 ♕c2

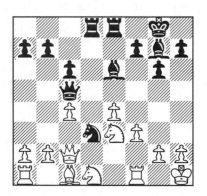

However, even the materialistic robot
appreciates that the gambit has worked

out nicely, thanks to the octopus knight
on d3 – now that's what I call an outpost – and the menacing forces lurking
ominously behind. Doubling rooks on
the d-file and blasting open the centre
with ...f7-f5 both spring to mind in the
diagram position.

17...♘bd3 18 ♗xd3 ♘xd3 19 ♕e2

19 ♕d2 looks odd and – not surprisingly – leaves White struggling after
19...♗h6!, introducing a new pin and
preparing to punish White for neglecting to utilise his dark-squared bishop.

19...♕b3!

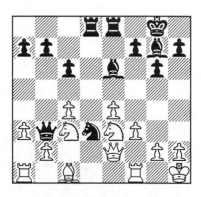

Black has such a commanding position that he might even contemplate
parting with the KID bishop by capturing on c3, regaining the pawn and
threatening another on c4. All this is
made possible thanks to the tremen-
dous outpost on d3, which White was
setting himself up for when accepting
the gambit on d6 and doing Black's job
for him by opening the d-file.

20 ♘cd1 ♖d7 21 ♖b1 ♖ed8

A dream position for Black, whose
every piece contributes to the terrible
bind in which White now finds himself.
Unfortunately the pressure now proves
too much for White, but his situation is

becoming untenable anyway...

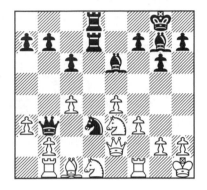

22 ♗d2?? ♘f4 0-1

Once again the initial uplifting feeling that accompanies the capture of a gambit pawn has given way to the realisation that factors other than material need to be taken into account.

Now for a Sicilian in which White facilitates an offensive against the enemy king with a gambit that frees a key centre square.

Ki.Georgiev-Sax
Reggio Emilia 1988

1 e4 c5 2 ♘f3 d6 3 d4 cxd4 4 ♘xd4 ♘f6 5 ♘c3 e6 6 g4

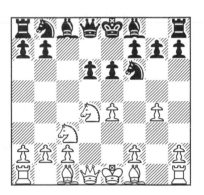

Here we go... White hopes to profit from his opponent's early adoption of the 'small' centre by launching a kingside attack.

6...h6 7 h4 ♘c6 8 ♖g1 h5 9 gxh5 ♘xh5 10 ♗g5 ♘f6 11 ♖g3

Keep an eye on this rook.

11...a6 12 ♘xc6 bxc6 13 ♕f3 ♗d7

A new move at the time, varying from 13...♖b8.

14 0-0-0 ♗e7

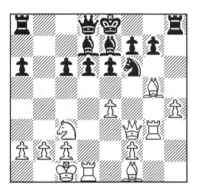

In typical Sicilian tradition the early skirmish in the opening has left Black's king without a natural safe haven, but he does have the b-file upon which to worry White's king, as well as a solid looking wall of pawns in the centre. How should White continue if he is to succeed in creating problems for his opponent?

15 e5!

A good practical approach. There's no point taking on the uncompromising Sicilian with the main line (2 ♘f3, 3 d4, 4 ♘xd4 etc.) if you're not willing to play in gambit style, and this dual-purpose gambit is exactly what White needed in the diagram position. As I have mentioned elsewhere in the book it is impossible to categorise every gambit, and the text, while freeing up the influential e4-square for White, also damages Black's central pawn complex and consequently puts the defender under pressure on the d-file.

15...dxe5

Forced.

16 ♘e4

The knight jumps to life on the useful e4-square, from where it exerts pressure on both d6 and f6, the latter factor in turn undermining the protection of the d7-bishop, no longer safely tucked in behind the small centre.

16...♖b8

There tends to be little time to consider the more deep and meaningful aspects of chess in some of the fiery lines of the Sicilian – hence White's well-timed gambit – and Black responds quickly by taking aim on the b-file. Georgiev's sacrifice stepped up the pace by creating an outpost in the middle of the arena, and it is the extra dimension(s) that the new square brings to White's attacking prospects that is significant rather than the identity of the piece that occupies it. Therefore after 16...♘xe4 17 ♕xe4 one good piece is replaced by a more powerful partner.

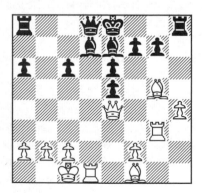

The queen is perfectly posted to oversee developments across the board. Then 17...f6? does not shut White out as 18 ♕g6+ ♔f8 19 ♗h6 lets him straight in. Instead there is 17...♗xg5+ 18 hxg5 ♕c7 19 ♖gd3 ♖d8 20 ♖d6

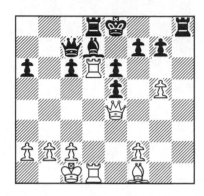

White sits comfortably in the driver's seat here, with at least a clear advantage.

17 ♗xf6 gxf6

Not 17...♗xf6? 18 ♖xg7!

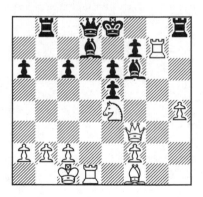

I assume Georgiev's gambit was in part inspired by this winner, which works because 18...♗xg7 leads to mate after 19 ♘d6+. Thus the capture with the pawn was forced, further compromising Black's defences.

18 ♕g2!!

As well as the brutally decisive ♖g8+

(when ...Rxg8 again leads to mate with the help of the knight), dropping the queen back also paves the way to swing the rook over to the d-file.

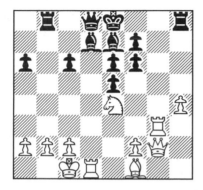

18...Rf8 19 Bc4! Qb6

Hoping to distract White by hitting b2. In the event of 19...Qa5 the knight plays a part thanks to a decoy sacrifice: 20 Ra3!! and now 20...Bxa3 21 Nxf6+ Ke7 22 Rxd7+ Kxf6 23 Qg5 is mate. Instead 20...Qb6 21 Rb3 leads back to the game, while White meets the retreat to c7 or d8 by doubling on the d-file. The attempt to bother the knight with 19...f5 walks into 20 Bxe6!!

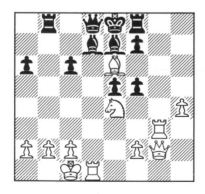

Ruthless. Gambit play and subsequent sacrifices often go hand in hand, particularly in these tense situations.

Now 20...fxe6 21 Rg7 threatens Qg6+, and after 21...Qb6 White finishes the job with 22 Rxe7+ Kxe7 23 Qg5+ and another starring role for the knight when it delivers mate on d6. Forced is 20...Bxe6 21 Rxd8+ Rxd8 22 Ng5, when White toys with the idea of sending the knight on another sortie to h7.

20 Rb3 Qa7 21 Rbd3 Rb7

Black has been reduced to passivity, allowing White to move in for the kill. Even the h-pawn is a potential problem for Black now that White is in charge of the kingside.

22 Qg7 f5

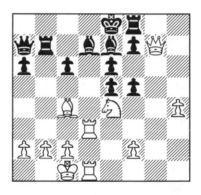

23 Nd6+!

The knight has proved useful in a number of variations thus far, and the check proves decisive.

23...Bxd6 24 Rxd6 Qxf2 25 Bxe6!

White has refused to take his foot off the pedal since parting with the e-pawn.

25...fxe6

25...Bxe6 26 Rd8+ is the point.

26 Rxd7 Qf4+ 27 Kb1 Rxb2+ 28 Kxb2 and now Black resigned rather than go through the motions with 28...Qb4+ 29 Kc1 Qa3+ 30 Kd2 Qb4+ 31 Ke2 and so on, when the king will soon escape.

Regardless of how much White had seen of the game (and of the numerous variations along the way) when he first embarked on the gambit theme, the point is that e4-e5 was enough to make a significant shift in the flow of the struggle, furnishing White with an initiative. This was made possible by the combination of the outpost on e4 (remember the vital role played by the knight once it relocated from c3), the d-file and Black's damaged kingside structure.

In order to balance out the small centre scenario here is an example in which it is Black who uses a gambit to establish a key outpost in the centre.

Shirov-J.Polgar
Buenos Aires 1994

1 e4 c5 2 ♘f3 e6 3 d4 cxd4 4 ♘xd4 ♘c6 5 ♘c3 d6 6 g4

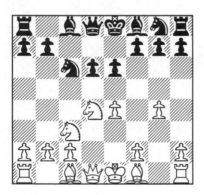

Thus far White has played exactly the same opening six moves as in the previous game, but this time Black has brought out his queen's knight instead. Consequently White has no target on f6. This is in fact a significant difference,

and Black comes up with an interesting gambit aimed at exploiting the fact that the knight is yet to leave g8.

6...a6 7 ♗e3 ♘ge7

From here on we have quite a different flavour from the previous example.

8 ♘b3 b5 9 f4

Shirov tries a different approach to his game with Salov from Linares in 1993, which went 9 ♕e2 ♘a5 10 0-0-0 ♘c4 11 f4 ♕c7 12 ♖d4 ♗b7 13 ♖xc4!? ♕xc4 14 ♕xc4 bxc4 15 ♗xc4 ♘c6 16 f5 ♘e5 17 ♘a5? (17 ♗e2 ♗e7 18 ♘a5 ♗c8 19 ♘a4 ♗d8 20 ♘b6 ♗xb6 21 ♗xb6 h5! is slightly better for Black according to Salov) 17...♘xc4 18 ♘xc4 ♖c8 19 ♘a5 ♖xc3 20 bxc3 ♗xe4 with a clear advantage for Black.

9...♗b7 10 ♕f3 g5!

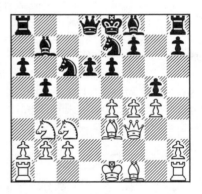

Another theoretical novelty, and quite an impressive one. Always be careful when advancing pawns for an offensive – they cannot move backwards. This is obvious but is nevertheless something that too many players fail to appreciate. Pawns leave behind potential weaknesses and – in this case – can be forcibly removed from their duties monitoring key squares. Having run the risk of overextending through his ambitious kingside play Shirov now finds himself with a positional predicament. Black's well timed decoy gambit is designed to undermine White's control of the dark squares and, in doing so, win the strategic battle for the influential e5-sqaure for her knight(s). The pawn offer does not guarantee an advantage for Black but at least it serves to break up the wall of pawns and fights for the initiative, and is a worthy alternative to the previously played 10...♞a5. Note that 10...b4? 11 ♞a4 ♞c8 12 0-0-0 helps only White.

11 fxg5

11 0-0-0 gxf4 12 ♗xf4 ♞g6 is the alternative. The e5-square looks like falling in Black's hands anyway, so Shirov decides to accept the gambit and perhaps put the new, advanced g-pawn to some use later in the game.

11...♞e5

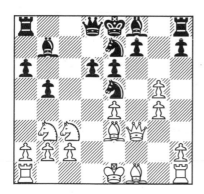

Mission accomplished (the first phase, at least). Whatever attacking plans White had when he raced his pawns forward will have to be revised or cancelled, for now the knight on e5 will need some watching. Ftacnik now investigates 12 ♕f6 offering the line 12...♞xg4 13 ♕xh8 ♞xe3 14 ♗d3 ♞g6,

e.g. 15 ♕f6 ♗e7 16 ♕f3 ♗xg5, or 15 ♕xh7 ♕xg5.

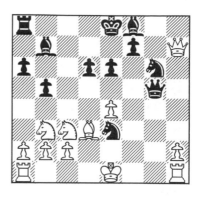

In both cases Black has justified the gambit with further investment, earning an additional outpost in the shape of the fantastic e3-square. Meanwhile the other knight is ready to hop into e5, and White has said goodbye to the dark squares. The text keeps the queen on home territory and stays in touch with the e4-pawn, which is not the case after 12 ♕e2 b4 13 ♞a4 ♗c6!? 14 ♞b6 ♗xe4 etc.

12 ♕g2 b4 13 ♞e2

Again Shirov looks to keep his game together. In the event of 13 ♞a4 Black might try 13...♞d5.

13...h5!!

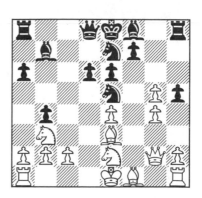

Striking while the iron is hot, Black endeavours to make more progress on the kingside. Now after 14 gxh6 ♗xh6 15 ♗xh6 (15 g5 ♘f5) 15...♖xh6 16 0-0-0 ♘7g6 Black has compensation for the pawn, while Ftacnik's suggestion of 16...♕b6 is also interesting.

14 gxh5?!

Opening the door a little too wide. Perhaps White should consider giving his king a shelter here with 14 0-0-0, although 14...hxg4 appears quite pleasant for Black.

14...♘f5!

Accepting the second gambit has presented Black with another great knight outpost.

15 ♗f2

Or 15 ♗f4 ♘h4 16 ♕g3 ♘hf3+ 17 ♔d1 ♗xe4

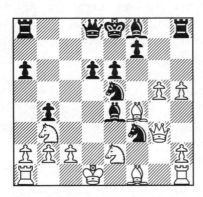

Black might still be a pawn down here but White's centre has disappeared completely and the king is awful. Black's knights seem to be causing major damage along with the b7-bishop so 15 exf5 ♗xg2 16 ♗xg2 comes to mind, but after 16...♖xh5 there remains a powerful knight on e5, and the sacrifice has not helped White. The text keeps the knight out of h4 but invites a more

dangerous piece into the game at a point when White is ill-equipped to defend.

15...♕xg5!

Exploiting her knights to great effect, the point being that after 16 ♕xg5 ♘f3+ 17 ♔d1 ♘xg5 Black is ready to win back the second of the gambit pawns with a clear advantage.

16 ♘ed4 ♘xd4 17 ♘xd4 ♖xh5 is good for Black, while there is also 16...♘h4!? 17 ♕xg5 ♘hf3+ 18 ♔d1 ♘xg5 etc. However, despite this being rather uncomfortable for White it is better than his next.

16 ♘a5? ♘e3!

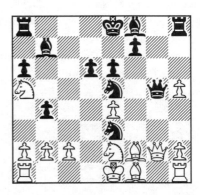

I wonder how much of these lines Black saw when taking over the initiative with the 10...g5 gambit? Well supported by the anchor on e5 as well as the b7-bishop, Black's second knight has made the decisive journey from e7 to e3, with a guaranteed win of material to follow.

17 ♕g3

17 ♗xe3 ♕xe3 18 ♘xb7 ♘f3+ wins the queen, while very entertaining and 'thematic' is the beautiful line 17 ♕xg5 ♘f3 mate with the following final position:

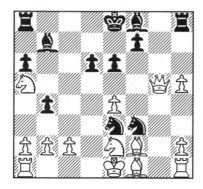

This is the kind of situation we might never have the (mis)fortune of experiencing, so it deserves a diagram even if we all saw it coming. Without the initial gambit Black would not have had the e5-square for the first knight, and without the second decoy gambit the f5-square would not have been available for its partner.

17...♕xg3 18 ♘xg3 ♘xc2+

Beginning a series of exchanges from which Black emerges with a decisive lead.

19 ♔d1

Or 19 ♔d2 ♘xa1 20 ♘xb7 ♗h6+ etc.

19...♘xa1 20 ♘xb7 b3

Black is an exchange up for no compensation.

21 axb3

21 a3 ♗h6 22 ♘xd6+ ♔d7.

21...♘xb3 22 ♔c2 ♘c5 23 ♘xc5 dxc5 24 ♗e1 ♘f3 25 ♗c3 ♘d4+ 26 ♔d3 ♗d6 27 ♗g2

Black had to check the following variation: 27 b4 ♔e7 28 bxc5 ♗xc5 29 ♗xd4 ♖hd8 30 ♘e2 ♗xd4 31 ♘xd4 e5.

27...♗e5 28 ♔c4 ♔e7 29 ♖a1 ♘c6 0-1

Ftacnik gives 30 ♔xc5 ♗xc3 31 bxc3 ♖hc8 32 ♔c4 ♘e5+ 33 ♔d4 f6 34 ♗f1 a5 as a possible continuation.

CHAPTER FIVE

Disruption

Apart from spilling your drink over the board or shouting 'Boo!' when your opponent is deep in thought, an excellent way of unsettling the opposition is with an unexpected gambit. Whether the result of such action is general disruption or 'mixing it' when prospects with normal play look bleak, the rewards can be considerable.

Fischer-Spassky
St Stefan/Belgrad (Match, G11) 1992

1 e4 c5 2 ♘f3 ♘c6 3 ♗b5 g6 4 ♗xc6 bxc6 5 0-0 ♗g7 6 ♖e1 e5 7 b4!?

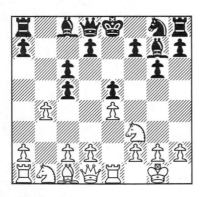

At the time of this match, which saw the great Bobby Fischer slip out of and back into the 'retirement' which began in the early 1970s, this gambit made its first appearance in international practice. Normally White continues 7 c3 ♘e7 8 d4 cxd4 9 cxd4 exd4 10 ♘xd4 0-0 11 ♘c3, which is enough for an edge for White. However, Fischer always liked to 'see them squirm' and here he welcomes the opportunity to knock his old rival off balance at the earliest opportunity.

7...cxb4 8 a3 c5

After the game it was agreed that by returning the pawn with 8...b3 Black could make life less uncomfortable for himself.

9 axb4 cxb4 10 d4

White simply won't let up on his quest for the dark squares.

10...exd4 11 ♗b2 d6 12 ♘xd4

What started as a closed centre has been all but demolished, and White's compensation cannot be disputed. For the price of a pawn White is way ahead in development, has well placed pieces, more space and, consequently, potential targets in Black's camp. In fact Black is struggling to avoid being clearly worse.

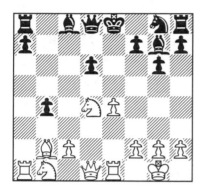

12...♕d7

In response to Spassky's suggested 12...♕b6 White has 13 ♘d2!, e.g. 13...♗xd4 14 ♘c4 ♗xf2+ 15 ♔h1 ♕c5 16 ♘xd6+ ♔e7 17 ♖f1 ♕xd6 18 ♕f3!

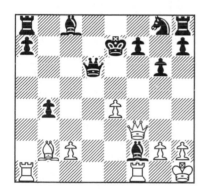

This is Timman's work, and the diagram position is nothing if not complicated. For the moment Black is two pieces up, but at least White seems to be having all the fun.

13 ♘d2 ♗b7?!

Black should deal with his kingside first with 13...♘e7. The text underestimates White's lead.

14 ♘c4 ♘h6

Again 14...♘e7 is a candidate, al-

though this time White has 15 ♘b5. After the text Black is just one move away from castling...

15 ♘f5!?

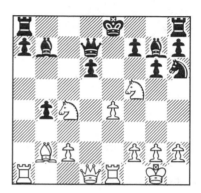

More interesting than 15 ♘b5.

15...♗xb2

Note that 15...♘xf5 16 exf5+ is check and White is close to winning after 16...♔f8 17 f6 ♗h6, e.g. 18 ♕xd6+ ♕xd6 19 ♘xd6 ♗c6 (19...♗d5? 20 ♖xa7!) 20 ♖e7.

16 ♘cxd6+ ♔f8 17 ♘xh6 f6?

It is understandable that Black would prefer to keep his bishop on the board here as his dark squares could be in trouble, but 17...♗xa1 has to be played, when 18 ♕xa1 ♕xd6 19 ♕xh8+ ♔e7 20 ♕xh7 ♕e6 this time leaves Black with compensation for a pawn according to Timman.

18 ♘df7! ♕xd1

18...♔e7 doesn't help Black: 19 ♘xh8 ♗xa1 20 ♕xa1 ♖xh8 21 e5 ♕c6 22 exf6+ ♔d7 23 f3 etc.

19 ♖axd1 ♔e7 20 ♘xh8 ♖xh8

Black is an exchange down but the two bishops and passed a-pawn might offer some chances. However, White's next nips any such hopes in the bud.

21 ♘f5+!!

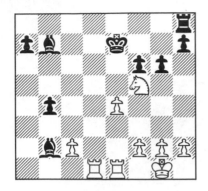

I guess White had this worked out all along. Just as a new phase of the game was about to begin White shows sufficient force to push his opponent back on the defensive, this time with decisive consequences.

21...gxf5

21...♔e6 22 ♖d6+ ♔e5 leads with the king but after 23 ♖d7 ♗c6 (23...♗xe4 24 ♘d6 ♔e6 25 ♖xa7) 24 ♖e7+ ♔f4 25 g3+ ♔g4 26 ♘e3+ ♔h5 27 ♖xa7 Black is lost.

22 exf5+ ♗e5 23 f4 ♖c8 24 fxe5

24 ♖d2 ♖c5 25 ♖de2 should also be enough to decide matters.

24...♖xc2 25 e6

Black is without hope now. The rest of the game went as follows: **25...♗c6 26 ♖c1 ♖xc1 27 ♖xc1 ♔d6 28 ♖d1+ ♔e5 29 e7 a5 30 ♖c1! ♗d7 31 ♖c5+ ♔d4 32 ♖xa5 b3 33 ♖a7 ♗e8 34 ♖b7 ♔c3 35 ♔f2 b2 36 ♔e3 ♗f7 37 g4 ♔c2 38 ♔d4 b1♕ 39 ♖xb1 ♔xb1 40 ♔c5 ♔c2 41 ♔d6 1-0**

In the next game White decides early on that his extra space afforded by the advanced e5-pawn will help in breaking through in the centre for an attack against Black's king. To this end he invites his opponent to enter into complications on the queenside.

Spassky-Reshko
Leningrad Championship 1959

1 e4 c6 2 ♘c3 d5 3 ♘f3 ♗g4 4 h3 ♗xf3 5 ♕xf3 ♘f6 6 e5 ♘fd7 7 ♕g3

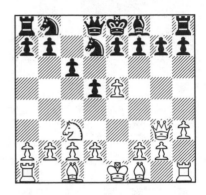

'Don't bring your queen out too early in the game' is good advice that is well worth following, particularly after seeing some of the examples in this book in which much time is lost when the queen starts taking gambit pawns. However, some systems justify a rapid deployment of the queen, and this is one of them. The first thing to notice when looking at the diagram position is that it is closed in nature, so the queen is safe from harassment. Apart from supporting the e5-pawn, from g3 there is another, more aggressive role in that by monitoring the g7-pawn White hinders the development of Black's kingside.

7...e6 8 ♗e2 ♕c7 9 f4 a6

Black wants to push the c-pawn without having to worry about ♘b5.

10 b4!?

Typical of the young Spassky, this

odd looking thrust – which appears to have no connection with what has developed on the kingside – seems to have as much psychological value as it does actual merit on the board. Black is first reminded that his bishop's current duty is to protect g7, so ...♗xb4 cannot be seriously considered. Otherwise, what is White trying to achieve on the queenside? Is the plan to capture the c-pawn when it arrives on c5? Evidently not.

10...c5

10...♗xb4, in fact, borrows an idea from a variation of the French Defence in which Black surrenders a couple of kingside pawns, so 11 ♕xg7 ♖f8 12 ♕xh7 c5 followed by ...♘c6 and ...0-0-0 is not completely illogical, but offers insufficient compensation nevertheless.

11 b5 c4 12 ♖b1

Hindsight is a valuable analytical tool but, given Spassky's credentials, this queenside strategy seems to be designed to lull Black into a false sense of confidence, to keep him busy winning the battle in this sector while White has plans to win the war elsewhere. Chess players can be a crafty bunch. Black has already indicated that a knight is unwel-

come on b5, so Spassky must have been expecting (hoping for?) his opponent's next.

12...d4 13 ♘e4

A nice outpost for the knight.

13...axb5

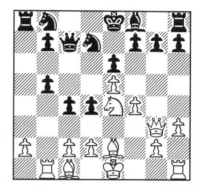

For the moment the b5-pawn is safe because its capture here meets with ...♕c6, hitting both rook and knight. So this is gambit play from White... Meanwhile, Black's latest introduces the threat to double the pawn tally with ...♖xa2. White is more interested in matters on the kingside which, for the moment, remains closed (and therefore safe for Black).

14 0-0 ♖xa2?!

A second pawn bites the dust, and another is now under fire on c2. Black can be forgiven for feeling confident, for assuming that White's strategy of practically surrendering the queenside is simply too risky. However, with one pawn already in the bag, and with the a-pawn not going anywhere, the sensible 14...♘c6 looks preferable from a practical point of view.

15 d3 ♖xc2 16 ♗d1 ♖a2

Black's domination of the queenside (White doesn't have much queenside remaining) is beyond dispute, but the risk in these situations is that greed rears its ugly head. I used the word 'practical' earlier, and this is because there is nothing seriously wrong with Black's play other than the fact that the unusual scenario is far more suited to White if we factor in style, psychology and – ultimately – talent. The soundness of White's gambit is less relevant than the possibilities it generates and how the players subsequently cope with them.

I once told GM Stuart Conquest how impressed I was with the attacking play of a junior in our charge at the World Youth Championships a few years ago, and he replied he was more interested in how the boy would manage when under pressure. It is this psychological appreciation that plays a major part in disruptive gambits. Here, for example, Black might contemplate letting the busy rook go with 16...cxd3, e.g. 17 ♗xc2 dxc2 18 ♖xb5 ♕c6 19 ♕d3 ♘c5 20 ♘xc5 ♗xc5 with a knight and (after the c-pawn falls) two pawns for the exchange and some simplification. However, Black is in material mode, concerned only with building up a points lead.

17 f5!

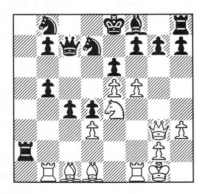

Finally. Let's take a look at this position and weigh up what return White has for his investment of three pawns. The development lead appears initially to be hardly noticeable, but each of White's queenside pieces is ready to jump into action despite sitting on the back rank. A good piece does not have to be posted in the middle of the board to play an effective role, it is enough to be within striking distance of the appropriate sector, and this describes all three of these pieces on b1, c1 and even d1. Meanwhile, the hitherto closed kingside is about to be opened up, and Black has been so busy collecting pawns on the other flank that he is vulnerable here. Moreover, Black is also ill-prepared to begin defending. But the flavour of the game is about to be spiced up, which is what White has been planning since around the time he teased his opponent with 10 b4.

17...♘xe5

Walking into a pin on the h2-b8 diagonal, but the line 17...♕xe5 18 fxe6 ♕xe6 19 ♖e1 opens the position very favourably for White, while 17...exf5 18 ♖xf5 and 19 e6, 19 ♖xf7 or 19 ♘d6+ is uncomfortable for the defender.

18 fxe6 f6

Bolstering the defence of the knight and shoring up the f-file, which does look preferable to 18...fxe6 19 ♗f4 ♘bd7 20 ♖xb5, when White finally recaptures the b5-pawn, and with some effect. Black is tied up, and 20...♖a5 21 dxc4 followed by 22 ♗g4 or 22 ♘g5 steps up the pace to another level and fully justifies the gambits. However, even after the text White will not be denied his attack on the king.

19 ♖xf6!

Yet another substantial sacrifice without which the gambit approach would have come to nothing. White's gambits were designed to engineer a situation in which attention would shift from the ostensibly messy queenside action to explosive play in the centre. Since material considerations have no part to play in gambit mode, nor should we concern ourselves with such matters when the sought after critical situation arrives.

19...gxf6 20 ♘xf6+ ♔d8 21 ♘d5 ♕d6

21...♕g7 runs into 22 e7+ ♔d7 23 ♗g4+ ♔e8 (23...♘xg4 24 ♕c7+) 24 ♗h5+.

22 ♗g5+ ♔c8

22...♔e8 23 ♗h5+ ♘g6 24 ♘c7+.

23 ♗g4

Threatening a nasty discovered check with e6-e7+ etc.

23...♘xg4

23...♗g7 addresses the threat but White has 24 ♘e7+ (24 e7+ ♘bd7) 24...♔c7 25 ♘f5 ♕xe6 26 ♘xg7 ♕d5 27 ♗f6 and Black cannot deal with both the pin and the discovered attack on the rook after ♘e6+. In reply to 23...♘bd7

a mate in one looms after 24 exd7+ ♘xd7 25 ♖e1!

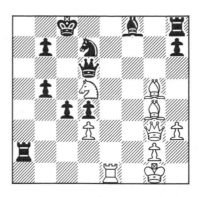

Then 25...b6 26 ♕f3 ♗g7 27 ♕f7 homes in with decisive effect, while pinning the rook with 25...♖a1 merely postpones the end: 26 ♗f4 ♕a6 27 ♘b6+ ♕xb6 28 ♖xa1 ♔d8 29 ♗g5+ etc. There is also 23...♕xd5 24 e7+ ♔c7 25 e8♕.

24 e7 ♗xe7

24...♖xg2+ 25 ♕xg2 ♗g7 26 ♕xg4+ ♘d7 27 ♖a1! and now 27...♔b8 meets with 28 ♕xd7! because 28...♕xd7 29 ♗f4+ cleans up. 24...♕xg3?? allows White to promote with mate.

25 ♕xg4+ ♘d7 26 ♘xe7+

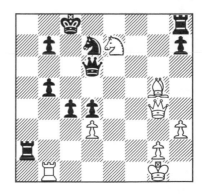

Wherever the king goes Black will lose too much.

26...♔c7 27 ♗f4 ♘e5 28 ♕g7 ♔b6 29 ♗xe5 ♕e6 30 ♗xd4+ 1-0

A common scenario for many players is to be struggling in a cramped position, see a means to rock the boat that costs a pawn or more, decide against parting with such a potentially decisive amount of material and, ultimately, watch the situation deteriorate until the loss is inevitable. Our results will improve, and our games will certainly be more interesting, when we start to give these gambit ideas a try. Here is such an example.

Anand-Kramnik
Wijk aan Zee 1998

1 e4 c5 2 ♘f3 ♘c6 3 d4 cxd4 4 ♘xd4 ♘f6 5 ♘c3 e5 6 ♘db5 d6

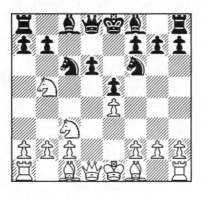

The Sicilian Sveshnikov voluntarily accepts a backward d-pawn, the accompanying hole on d5 and – in the main lines – doubled f-pawns in return for uncompromising play in complex positions.

7 ♗g5 a6 8 ♘a3 b5 9 ♗xf6 gxf6

The new f-pawn has a future with ...f6-f5 in these lines, which revolve around activity.

10 ♘d5 ♗g7 11 ♗d3 ♘e7 12 ♘xe7 ♕xe7 13 0-0 0-0 14 ♕f3!?

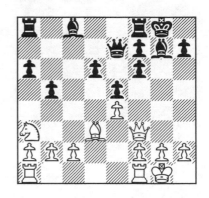

After trading in his dark-squared bishop to eliminate a key defender of the d5-square White seeks to clamp down on d5 and f5. Given time White will play c2-c3 and relocate the currently quiet knight with ♘c2-e3, from where yet more pressure can be exerted on d5 and f5. In fact this could quickly turn into a nightmare for Black, particularly when ♘d5 ....♗xd5, e4xd5 clears the b1–h7 diagonal for White's bishop, for example. Despite this unattractive prospect, most club players would not address it until later in the game when it might be too late. This policy holds little promise indeed.

Looking at the diagram position, what do you think might be the consequences of pawn breaks involving ...f6-f5 and/or ...d6-d5 in conjunction with ....♗b7 and perhaps ...e5-e4 thrown in for good measure? The closer we look the more attractive this kind of disruption becomes and, furthermore, disruption could well be the appropriate word because White's poor knight leaves him less able to cope with a change in pace...

14...f5!?

Black has the bishop pair, bishops need open lines, and modest play runs the risk of slipping into passivity and seeing the weak squares and pawns dominated. Put that way, Kramnik's gambit strategy could be considered the least risky option.

15 exf5 d5!

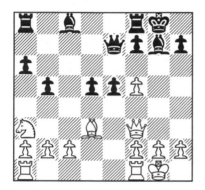

A gambit is a gambit, so don't be afraid to add to your investment if it means generating maximum compensation. 15...♗b7 is tempting in view of 16 ♗e4 d5 17 ♗xd5 e4 but White hits back with 18 f6! ♗xf6 19 ♕g3+ ♗g7 20 ♗xb7 ♕xb7 21 c3, emerging with a safe extra pawn.

16 ♕xd5

Otherwise the rather worrying ...e5-e4 is coming.

16...♗b7 17 ♕b3 e4

Black has let two pawns go, it must be said, but in return his bishops now criss-cross the board and White has been pushed back, and Black controls more of the centre. Also possible is 17...♖fd8 18 ♖fd1 ♖d4 19 ♗f1!, when 19...♖b4 backfires after 20 ♖d7! and the black queen has suddenly become overloaded.

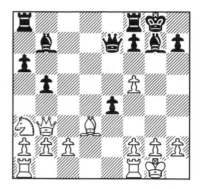

18 ♗e2 ♕g5!

Taking up a menacing post and introducing a dangerous possibility (see the next note).

19 ♖ad1!

White would like to exploit the location of his queen and return the knight to the fold with 19 ♘c4 but then Black has 19...e3!!

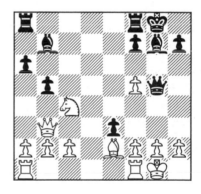

The point of this third gambit is not the obvious threat of mate in one but the less obvious trouble White experiences after 20 f3? ♗d5 21 ♕xe3 ♕xe3+, when 22 ♘xe3 ♗d4 23 ♔f2 ♖fe8 wins for Black. This leaves 20 ♘xe3 ♖ae8 and White is under pressure, e.g. 21 g3 ♗d4 22 h4 ♕h6 23 ♖ad1 ♗xe3 24 fxe3 ♖xe3 25 ♖d6, when 25...♖xe2 26 ♖xh6

♖g2+ 27 ♔h1 ♖f2+ 28 ♔g1 ♖g2+ leads to a draw, while 25...♗xb3!? 26 ♖xh6 ♖xg3+ 27 ♔f2 ♖g2+ 28 ♔e1 f6! is an attempt for more in view of the almost trapped rook on h6.

White can also try to relieve some of the pressure by giving a pawn back with 21 h4 ♕xh4 22 ♖fe1 (22 ♖fd1 ♗h6!), and now 22...♖e4!?, intending ...♖b4, invites White to react with 23 g3??

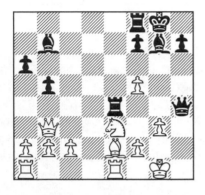

Is it time to retreat? No: 23...♕h1+!! 24 ♔xh1 ♖h4+ 25 ♔g1 ♖h1 mate.

Another option is 22...♗d4! with the idea of meeting 23 ♗f1 with 23...♗e5! when White is struggling for survival. Regardless of possible improvements (for both sides), the important feature in these lines is the transformation of Black's prospects from passive to rather promising. By 'mixing it' at the cost of a few pawns Black has managed to reverse the roles in terms of who is in charge, something that has additional psychological advantages.

19...e3 20 f3

Now there is an advanced passed pawn for White to worry about, but 20 g3? ♖ae8 21 ♘c4 exf2+ 22 ♖xf2 ♖xe2! 23 ♖xe2 ♕g4 favours Black.

20...♗e5

20...♔h8 21 ♘c4 sees the knight emerge from the wilderness, while taking time out to collect the f5-pawn with 20...♕xf5 justifies 21 c4. The text brings another piece to a more dangerous post.

21 ♘c4!

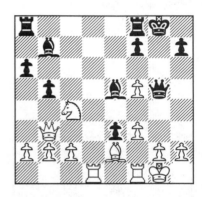

Impressive defence. The point is that after (and very well done of you found this one...) 21...bxc4? 22 ♕xb7 ♕h4 23 f4 ♗xf4? 24 g3 ♗xg3 White has 25 ♕g2.

21...♗f4 22 ♖d4

22 ♘d6? ♕h6 and Black hits d6 and h2.

22...♗d5!?

This is the kind of move we see occasionally see adorned with '!!?' for nerve/entertainment value. Instead 22...♖ad8! is playable. Then after 23 ♖fd1 ♗d5! the situation is different from the game. This time 24 ♖xf4 ♕xf4 25 ♕xe3 ♕xf5 26 ♗d3 ♕e6 (26...♕f6) 27 ♕g5+ ♔h8 28 ♕h4 f5 29 ♕d4+ ♔g8 leaves White no time for 30 ♘e3? in view of 30...♗xf3. Instead 24 ♖xd5 ♖xd5 25 ♖xd5 ♕h4 26 g3! (26 ♘xe3? ♗xe3+ 27 ♕xe3 ♕e1+ picks up the queen after 28 ♗f1 ♕xe3+) 26...♗xg3 27 ♕xe3 ♕xh2+ 28 ♔f1 ♕h3+ 29 ♔g1 ♕h2+ 30 ♔f1 ♕h3+ leads to a draw.

23 ♖xf4

White tidies up. 23 ♖xd5 ♛h4

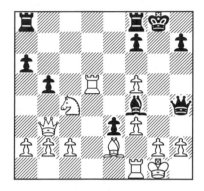

24 g3 ♗xg3 25 hxg3 ♛xg3+ 26 ♔h1 ♛h3+ 27 ♔g1 heads towards a draw even if Black tries for more: 27...♔h8!? 28 ♛c3+ f6 29 ♘xe3 ♖g8+ 30 ♘g4 ♛g3+ 31 ♔h1 ♛h3+ etc. White has an opportunity to go wrong with the natural 23 g3? ♗xc4 24 ♗xc4 bxc4 25 ♛xc4 e2! etc.

23...♛xf4

After 23...♗xc4? 24 ♛xe3! ♖fe8 25 ♛c1! Black walks into ♖g4(+).

24 ♛xe3 ♛xf5 25 ♗d3 ♛f6

25...♛e6 26 ♛g5+! ♔h8 27 ♛h4, e.g. 27...f5 28 ♛d4+ ♔g8 29 ♘e3! ♖ad8 30 ♘xf5!.

26 ♘b6

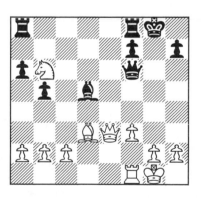

White has dealt well with his opponent's disruptive tactics, succeeding in cutting a path through the jungle of threats to emerge with a couple of pawns for the exchange and a solid set-up.

26...♖ad8 27 ♘xd5 ♖xd5 28 ♛e4 ♛d4+ 29 ♛xd4 ♖xd4 30 ♖e1 ½-½

The bishop is a big piece.

Now for another vintage Spassky performance, this time refusing to be thrown by a cheeky attack on his bishop, instead producing a gambit of two pawns that leaves Black's king stranded in the centre. Often when this happens the unfortunate king comes under rapid fire, but here White ruthlessly concentrates on accentuating the inconvenience experienced by Black.

Spassky-Witkowski

Riga 1959

1 d4 ♘f6 2 c4 g6 3 ♘c3 d5 4 cxd5 ♘xd5 5 e4 ♘xc3 6 bxc3 ♗g7 7 ♗c4

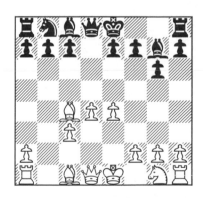

7...c5

This thrust is a key characteristic of the Exchange Grunfeld and will come sooner or later, but more common is the immediate 7...0-0 8 ♘e2 c5. In view of what happens Black must have regretted his less popular order of moves.

8 ♘e2 cxd4 9 cxd4 ♘c6 10 ♗e3 b5 11 ♗d5!

11 ♗xb5?! is a little too accommodating: 11...♕a5+ 12 ♘c3 ♕xc3+ 13 ♗d2 ♕xd4 14 ♗xc6+ ♗d7 15 ♗xa8 ♕xa1 looks like an artificial series of exchanges but is quite well known and leads to equality.

11...♗d7 12 ♖c1

12 ♗xc6 ♗xc6 13 d5 ♗d7 14 ♗d4 is also possible.

12...♖c8 13 0-0

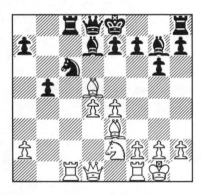

13...e6

Black addresses the plan of trading on c6 followed by gaining space with d4-d5. Perhaps he was not satisfied with the compensation after 13...0-0 14 ♗xc6 ♖xc6 15 ♖xc6 ♗xc6 16 d5 ♗d7 17 ♗xa7 ♕a5 18 ♗c5 ♕xa2 19 ♗xe7 ♖c8, with the bishop pair, active forces and a passed pawn to show for the pawn. White has a passed pawn of his own and no weaknesses, but the situation is not clear. I wonder how the fiery Spassky would have handled being on the receiving end of this gambit.

14 ♗xc6 ♖xc6

In the event of 14...♗xc6 White gets away with 15 d5! exd5 16 exd5 because 16...♕xd5 leaves the bishop pinned after 17 ♕xd5, and 16...♗xd5 loses to 17 ♖xc8 ♕xc8 18 ♕xd5. Therefore 16...♗b7 is forced, when 17 ♗c5 ♕xd5 18 ♘f4 ♕xd1 19 ♖fxd1 catches Black's king in the centre. By recapturing on c6 with the rook first Black avoids these problems.

15 ♖xc6 ♗xc6 16 d5!?

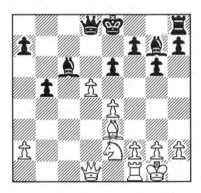

It is quite an unpleasant sensation to prevent an idea only to see it played out before you anyway, and in this case Black – no doubt ready to castle next move – now has to recalculate the implications of this advance. Clearly White does not intend to grab the a7-pawn.

16...exd5 17 ♕c2

Gaining a tempo and freeing d1 for the rook.

17...♕d7

Stahlberg-Jimenez Zerquera, Marianske Lazne 1965 went 17...♗b7 18 ♕c5 ♕b6 19 ♕b4 a5 20 ♕d2 d4 21 ♘xd4 0-0 22 ♘f5 ♕d8 23 ♘d6 with a pull for White, although he surrendered his great knight and any hopes of an advantage after 23...♕d7 24 ♘xb7 ♕xb7 25

♕xa5 ♖a8 26 ♕b4 ♖xa2 with a draw. Instead Black would have hesitated to remove the influential knight with his other bishop because this would have handed over the dark squares. White can also continue as in the main game with 18 ♗c5.

18 ♗c5

The point. Whatever plans Black would obviously have featured the traditionally desirable ...0-0, so now it is time for Plan B. However, what we are concerned with here is that the position in front of us is the foundation of White's Plan A, and herein lies one of the secrets of the disruptive gambit – create your own rules at the expense of the opposition.

18...dxe4 19 ♖d1 ♕b7

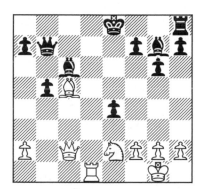

The gambit was always going to involve parting with two pawns but, like so many of the examples in these pages, whether it be one, two or even three pawns should have no influence on selecting the strategy in the first place. Either we get something tangible for the gambit or we don't – the price is irrelevant. In the diagram position Black would be doing more than fine were it not for his hapless king, so it is impera-

tive that White maintains the bind. In doing so he is effectively playing with an extra rook, a factor so significant that it is far more noticeable than the pawn count.

20 ♘d4

Another problem for Black is the importance of his dark-squared bishop, without which Black's defensive task would be practically impossible to deal with. Consequently White is able to operate with either minor piece on the dark squares in the knowledge that a trade involving the g7-bishop leaves him with an 'extra' piece against the powerless (in terms of the dark squares) bishop.

20...♗e5

It is difficult to see how Black can keep White at bay. For example after 20...♗d7 21 ♘b3 f5 (preparing ...♔f7 and liberty for the rook) 22 ♕d2 ♕c6 23 ♗b4 ♗e5? 24 ♘d4! ♕f6 25 ♘f3! White wins. Acquiescing immediately with 20...♗xd4 21 ♖xd4 f5 invites a powerful infiltration with 22 ♖d6 etc.

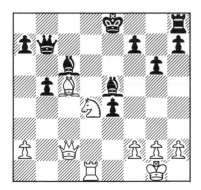

21 ♗b4 ♗xd4

From here on in White will make sure that the battle is fought exclusively on the dark squares, thus making

Black's bishop superfluous. After 21...♗d7 22 ♕c5 ♗f6 23 ♕d6 ♕b6 (23...♗d8 24 ♕e5+) 24 ♕d5 Black's defences begin to give way.

22 ♖xd4

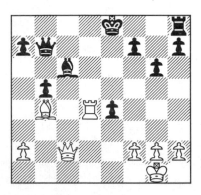

Not only has the fate of Black's king failed to improve, he has now practically surrendered the dark squares. Meanwhile the rook remains powerless in the corner, in contrast to White's.

22...a5 23 ♗c5

23 ♕c5 f6 (23...axb4 24 ♕e5+) 24 ♖d6 is tempting but backfires on White, e.g. 24...0-0 25 ♖d7 ♖c8!, or 25 ♖xc6 axb4 26 ♖c7 ♖d8 27 h4 ♕d5 28 ♕a7 ♕d1+ 29 ♔h2 ♕d6+ 30 g3 ♕f8. However, Spassky's 24 ♗xa5 ♔f7 25 ♖d6 ♖c8 26 ♗c3 is something for White despite the entrance of Black's rook. Anyway, the text is the consistent choice, keeping the vice firmly in place.

23...♕c8 24 h3!

Not the first time such a quiet, unassuming move carries such venom. White now threatens to take on e4, which would be faulty immediately in view of 24 ♖xe4+? ♗xe4 25 ♕xe4+ ♕e6, when 26 ♕a8+ ♔d7 27 ♕xh8?? ♕e1 mate turns the tables.

24...f5

Or 24...f6 25 ♕b3 a4 26 ♕b2

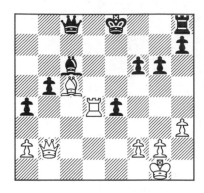

Now 26...h5 (followed by ...♖h7) should be met with 27 ♖d1! ♔f7 28 ♖d6 rather than 27 ♖d6, which obstructs the bishop and allows Black to finally castle into relative safety.

25 ♕b2 ♗d7

25...♖g8 26 ♖d6 is decisive.

26 ♖xe4+ fxe4 27 ♕xh8+ ♔f7 28 ♕xh7+ ♔f6

28...♔e6 29 ♕e7+ ♔f5 30 g4+ ♔f4 31 ♕d6+ is the game.

29 ♕e7+ ♔f5

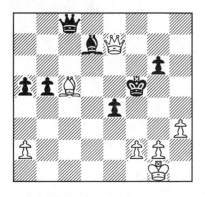

Note how White has succeeded in operating only on the dark squares.

30 g4+ ♔f4 31 ♕d6+ ♔g5

Or 31...♔f3 32 ♕d1+ ♔f4 33 ♕d2+.

32 ♗e3+ 1-0

CHAPTER SIX

Structure

While it is quite easy to identify and appreciate standard structural characteristics that might prove problematic for their owner – such as isolated, backward and doubled pawns – we tend, however, to shy away from parting with material in order to inflict upon the opponent such a positional handicap. Most of the time this kind of structural damage comes about as a result of exchanges of pieces in which pawns are involved, or captures that leave surviving pawns isolated or backward, for example. In other words these situations might be created almost by accident, a positional bonus at the end of a series of moves or strategy that had another purpose. But if we rub our hands in anticipation of how our structural superiority will help when it appears at no cost, there is no reason why we shouldn't be prepared to pay a price for a significant advantage. Here are a few examples of positionally oriented gambits that have specific structural aims as their foundation. Often this breaking up of the opponent's structure has an element of disruption to it as well.

Bronstein-Tartakower
Saltsjobaden Interzonal 1948

1 e4 c6 2 ♘f3 d6 3 d4 ♗g4 4 h3!

'The bishop is stronger than the knight' – Bronstein.

4...♗h5 5 ♗e3 ♘f6 6 ♘bd2 ♘bd7 7 c3 ♗g6

Black hopes to profit from his 'extra' development of the bishop, but the time taken indulging this piece (three tempi) presents White with a gambit possibility which results in entombing the other bishop!

8 e5 ♘d5 9 e6!?

Gambits, of course, can result in

compensation or advantages of one or more form, and the text, while in the long term being positionally (structurally) motivated, does have the effect of setting Black development problems. Normally ...e7-e6 or ...e7-e5 would be played, followed by ...♗e7 and ...0-0, but with two e-pawns this won't be easy. A fianchetto is out of the question because the g-pawn is obstructed by the other bishop. White, on the other hand, can mobilise with ease.

Then we can turn to the structural implications of White's gambit. Under most circumstances doubled pawns can be trouble, but this is particularly the case when they appear unexpectedly, when they are not part of the plan. In order to avoid being too cramped Black will have to push with ...e6-e5, when a trade will result in the doubled pawns also being isolated (after ...d6xe5), thus compounding the positional problem.

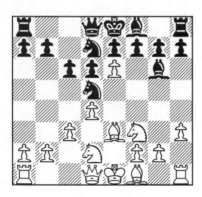

9...fxe6 10 ♗e2 e5 11 dxe5 ♘xe5

Black takes the opportunity to win some breathing space with an exchange of knights.

12 ♘xe5 dxe5

A good guide for students, when making a positional evaluation, is to count the number of pawn islands (the fewer the better). Here the e-pawns stand out, but you must have noticed that Black can redress the balance in these terms with ...♘xe3, when f2xe3 leaves White with an isolated pawn. Of course Bronstein had factored this into his overall game-plan, as we will see, suffice to say that a successful maintenance of a new e-pawn would hold back both black e-pawns, to a certain extent nullifying the difference in points. Meanwhile, in the diagram position, it is clear that Black's best bishop is the one on g6, a piece which also keeps guard over the possibly useful e4-square. Consequently White's next is quite logical.

13 ♗h5!

13 ♗g4 targets the wrong square and permits Black to return the pawn in favourable circumstances with 13...e6!, when 14 ♗xe6 ♕f6 15 ♗g4 ♘xe3 16 fxe3 ♗c5 sees Black come out fighting. By now there should be no need to remind you – but I will do so anyway – that, during a gambit phase, we should constantly be on the lookout for ways the opposition can improve his lot by giving back material.

13...♘xe3

Of course Black would prefer not to have a second set of doubled, isolated pawns, but the alternative 13...♗xh5 looks poor after 14 ♕xh5+ g6 15 ♕xe5, e.g. 15...♘f6 16 ♘e4 ♗g7 17 ♖d1! ♕b8 18 ♘xf6+ ♗xf6 19 ♕e6 ♕c8 20 ♕b3 or 15...♖g8 16 0-0-0, when Black suffers on more than one level.

14 ♗xg6+ hxg6 15 fxe3 ♕d3 16 ♕f3 e6

Since the previous diagram Black's structure has worsened somewhat, while White – as predicted – now has a new e-pawn. In the excellent *The Sorcerer's Apprentice*, Bronstein writes (many years later): 'Black has defended with great skill and now White has to make decision whether to put a knight on e4 or to castle queenside. Today, after half a century of experience, I would have chosen one of these moves but at that time I was proud to make a purely technical move after which, I was sure, I could not lose...'

So White would not have been surprised if, during the rest of the game, Black succeeded in protecting his weak pawns while holding things together elsewhere. However, the nature of these positional liabilities is such that they tend to be permanent (obviously) and, while they may survive for long periods, could come under fire at any time. Furthermore, there is very little one can do with doubled, isolated pawns, and this severe loss in flexibility and choice tends to have implications in other areas of the board and stages of the game. Whatever assessment we make of the current position in real terms, practically the onus is on Black to keep his eyes well peeled and to tread carefully, and this is never easy – regardless of a player's strength.

17 ♕e4 ♕xe4 18 ♘xe4 ♗e7 19 ♔e2!

With the game having quickly undergone a transformation, the opening phase has given way to the (late) middlegame, with the remaining combination of forces in play suggesting that we will soon be in the ending. Consequently it makes little sense for White to castle here given that the king is in no danger, and from e2 it is ready to act on either flank should the need arise. With White's knight ideally located on e4 this game could quite easily have been slotted into the Outposts chapter, while the initial disrupting effect of the gambit would not be out of place under the Disruption heading. Each facet of the gambit deserves its own appreciation, and here the respective structures make for interesting viewing. Anyway, White's knight soon hands over the e4-square to the pawn.

19...♖d8 20 ♖ad1 0-0 21 ♖xd8 ♖xd8 22 ♖f1

Cutting off Black's king which, like White's, would be better posted nearer the centre. The good thing about sitting on White's side of the board in this kind of position is the reassurance that the enemy weaknesses provide a not inconsiderable helping of hope for the future. That four pawns are so powerless in terms of defence that 'outside' protection is required for their survival is something that Black needs to stay aware of at all times. A decision concerning events that are essentially unrelated could have serious consequences to the foot soldiers. And since these pawns are so near and yet so far, so to speak, the fall of one might lead to the fall of the next. The psychological impact of such responsibility can be rather debilitating. Incidentally, I have noticed that the publication of my *Chess Psychology* in 2003 – a book of which I am quite proud, you understand – is having a positive effect on my chess thinking. How we and our opponents cope psychologically with this or that aspect is very important, particularly in gambit play, and this area of the game merits investigation. With this in mind, we can appreciate that Black now looks to the queenside for some relief.

22...b6?!

Adding protection to the c5-square

(for the moment the bishop defends, but otherwise ♘c5 hits both b7 and e6). However, this weakens the c6-pawn, prompting White to relocate his knight to the queenside.

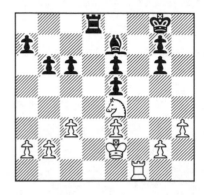

23 ♘f2 ♖d5

There are very few pieces on the board and Black seems to be holding his ramshackle position together, but planless moves easily run into trouble. For example 23...♗f6?, hoping to shore up the kingside, invites 24 ♘g4, when the forced 24...♖f8 surrenders the d-file. After 25 ♖d1! White is ready to bring his king to e4 (via f3), for instance. Perhaps 23...♗d6 is possible. Instead Black activates his rook.

24 ♘d3 ♗f6 25 ♘b4

White's last three moves highlight the knight's versatility. The ability to change course and operate (attack/defend) on both colour complexes is surprisingly under-used by most players. Even a conventionally ideally placed piece can be improved, but we tend to look for or find these possibilities easier with bishops (which move directly within a finite area) than with knights. The text is another example of 'wishing' a piece to a better (perhaps temporary) square and then seeing whether it can realistically reach the target. By the way, remember that White, now whittling away at the queenside, is still a pawn down.

25...♖b5

25...♖d6 26 ♖d1 ♖xd1 27 ♔xd1 c5 28 ♘c6 a5.

26 a4 ♖c5 27 e4!

Despite permanently removing a dream square for the knight this is both positionally and tactically justified. Tactically, Black was apparently planning 27...a5 here, the point being that after 28 ♘d3 ♖c4 Black picks up a pawn. However, White has instead the clever 28 ♔d3! (threatening ♘a6) 28...axb4 29 cxb4 and the rook is trapped.

27...b5 28 a5 ♗d8 29 ♖a1 ♖c4 30 ♔d3 ♗e7 31 ♘a6!

Suddenly Black's rook is in hot water thanks to the now greedy threat of b2-b3. Consequently Black's next is forced, after which the state of health of his pawns reaches a new low.

31...♖a4 32 ♖xa4 bxa4 33 ♘b8

Bronstein: 'Black's pawns do not support each other because they are disconnected and it is only a matter of time before the white knight gobbles up all the black pawns. The problem of

keeping seven pawns alive, all completely isolated, some doubled, could not even be solved by the ingenious brain of Dr Tartakower.' Precisely.

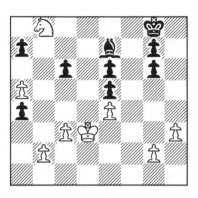

It is true that we find ourselves in an ending (although quite a bit of opening theory nowadays goes further than our journey thus far), but the important theme in the latest diagram position is the very same that White initiated with his gambit. It is fitting, then, that now each of Black's seven(!) pawns cannot be protected by another. The rest of the game is easy for White.

33...a3

33...c5 34 ♘c6 drops the a7-pawn.

34 bxa3 ♗xa3 35 ♘xc6 ♗c5 36 ♔c4

White wastes no time heading for the final obstacle.

36...♗g1 37 ♔b5 ♔f7 38 ♔a6 ♔f6 39 ♘xa7 ♔g5 40 g3

White has a choice of wins.

40...♗f2 41 c4 ♔f6 42 ♘c8 ♗xg3 43 c5 1-0

White's exploitation of structural features in the following game seems unusual, but in fact it flows from the time he uncorks the gambit.

Kramnik-Topalov
Dortmund 1999

1 d4 ♘f6 2 ♘f3 d5 3 c4 c6 4 ♘c3 a6

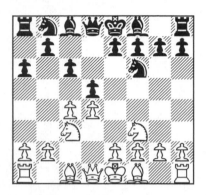

One of the trendy lines of the modern game, the '...a6 Slav' is a surprisingly rich alternative to the standard and hitherto automatic 4...dxc4. It is interesting that Kramnik's response is the most committal at his disposal, already laying the structural foundation on the queenside.

5 c5 ♗f5 6 ♗f4 ♘bd7 7 e3 e6 8 ♗e2 ♗e7 9 ♘d2!?

This seems to have been a new idea at the time. White tends to play the useful h2-h3 to give the bishop an escape square on h2 in case ...♘h5 comes. The text reduces White's control over e5 but rules out ...♘h5, while it also addresses one of Black's standard plans by introducing an effective positional (structural) possibility. Furthermore, in the more immediate future, dropping the knight back actually contains some venom.

9...♗g6

Black correctly judges that 9...0-0 10 g4 ♗g6 11 h4 might be too much fun for White, so he bides his time until White makes a decision regarding his own king.

10 b4

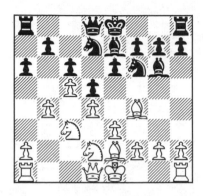

Thanks to the fixed pawns White has an easy to play plan of simply using his space advantage to launch a pawn offensive, Black's defensive task compounded by the fact that ...b7-b6 leaves the backward c6-pawn rather weak after c5xb6. Meanwhile, White's strong bishop on f4 rules out ...♖b8, so Black now sets about contesting the h2-b8 diagonal.

10...♕c8 11 0-0 ♗d8

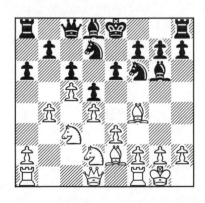

12 ♖c1!

Aware of White's plan, most players would consider 12 a4 to be the most consistent follow-up, but after 12...♗c7 13 ♗xc7 ♕xc7 14 f4 (otherwise ...e6-e5 comes) Black can get away with 14...b6, which is not the case after Kramnik's safety measure, reminding his opponent that opening the c-file is a risky venture when the rook and queen occupy the same file.

12...♗c7 13 ♗xc7 ♕xc7 14 f4

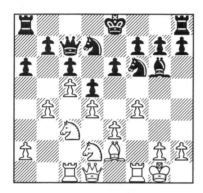

The main idea behind 9 ♘d2, and another structural commitment. However, in order to make anything of his space on the queenside White needs to nip in the bud any counterplay in the centre (the thematic reaction to play on the flanks).

14...♘g8

Again Black is careful not to castle into an attack: 14...0-0 15 g4 h6 16 h4 is as dangerous as it looks. Topalov's idea is to relocate the knight on e7, which has the advantage of freeing the f-pawn for a future ...f7-f6 and ...e6-e5 etc. With this in mind, White acts immediately.

15 e4 ♘e7

Black's last means that 15...dxe4 16 ♘dxe4 is not possible in view of the inconvenience the knight will cause when arriving on d6.

16 f5!?

Kramnik in the excellent *Kramnik: My Life and Games* writes 'A very risky decision that was not obligatory, but I wanted to make the play sharper.' From a psychological point of view the rest of the game takes a course (in the main) of White's choosing.

16...exf5 17 exd5

White is happy to give his opponent a 4-2 pawn majority on the kingside as long the queenside initiative gains momentum. The key difference lies in the structures – on the queenside White's is sound, advanced and has the potential to cause some damage, while Black's is fragile; on the kingside Black is in no position to get moving.

17...cxd5

17...♘xd5 18 ♘c4! is very much in White's favour, e.g. 18...0-0 19 ♘xd5 cxd5 20 ♘d6 with a clear advantage to White according to Kramnik or 18...♘xc3 19 ♖xc3 0-0 20 d5 etc.

18 b5!

Exploiting Black's king position (18...axb5 19 ♘xb5 and 20 ♘d6+) to further fix the queenside pawns.

18...0-0 19 b6 ♕d8

Kramnik suggests 19...♕c8 to protect the b7-pawn. This pawn might seem in no danger now, but it is in fact the weakness upon which White's strategy is based. The gambit with f4-f5 served to undermine the support of the d5-pawn, delegating the role exclusively to the c6-pawn, which now finds itself on d5. Consequently Black's queenside structure presents White with an effective long-term plan.

20 ♘b3 ♘f6 21 ♘a5 ♖b8 22 a4 ♘e4

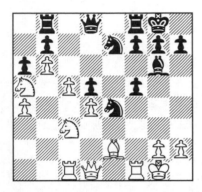

Kramnik: 'Initially I had been intending to sacrifice a piece here – 23 ♘xb7 ♖xb7 24 a5, and after 24...♘c6 25 ♕a4! Black cannot maintain the blockade on the queenside, but on approaching close to this position I saw that Black has counterplay, for example 24...f4!? 25 ♗xa6 ♖b8 26 ♘xe4 dxe4 27 c6 ♘xc6 28 ♖xc6 f3. Therefore for the moment the white knight is transferred to b4.'

23 ♘a2 f6?

23...f4! is a thematic counter-sacrifice, e.g. 24 ♖xf4 ♘f5 25 ♕d3 ♕g5 26 ♖cf1 ♖fe8 (26...♘fg3!?) 27 ♗d1 with an unclear position. However, Kramnik writes: 'This idea did not appeal to Topalov, and he preferred passive defence while retaining his extra material' – Remember that top players, too, find it

difficult to let go of their material lead, even if this means achieving some kind of counterplay to relieve the pressure of a difficult situation.

24 ♘b4 ♗e8 25 ♕c2!

By now you might have cottoned on to the fact that White is gradually building up to a full-scale battering of Black's static queenside. The text is 'essentially the key' according to Kramnik, who gives 25 ♘xb7 ♖xb7 26 ♗xa6 ♖xb6! (26...♖b8) 27 cxb6 ♕xb6 28 ♗b5 ♗xb5 29 axb5 ♕xb5 when the game 'should end in a draw' or 26 a5 ♘c6 27 ♗xa6 ♖e7 28 ♘xc6 ♗xc6 and the desirable plan of ♖b1 and ♗b5 to challenge the blockader is not on due to ...♘c3. Hence the patient ♕c2!

Breaking down ostensibly complex situations in this simple fashion is quite a gift, particularly when it is done at the board, under the tense conditions thrust upon us in the context of a tournament.

25...g6

In response to the more combative 25...g5!? Kramnik intended 26 ♗d3 to hold back – if only temporarily – Black's pawns and thus win time to pile on more pressure on the queenside.

26 ♖b1 ♖f7

'Black's problem is that it is hard for him to find a useful move' – Kramnik.

27 ♘xb7!

And it here it comes. I have no doubt that this idea was – in some form – on Kramnik's mind when he set the ball rolling with the gambit. It was important to first fix the queenside by pushing the b-pawn as far as it could go, but this was not difficult under the circumstances. White's resultant territorial supremacy and Black's creaking pawns were the other crucial factors.

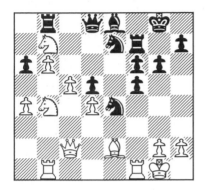

27...♖xb7 28 a5 ♘c6 29 ♘xc6 ♗xc6 30 ♗xa6 ♖b8 31 ♗b5!

Three connected passed pawns supported by major pieces make a force to be reckoned with, so this challenge is an important contributor to the success of White's strategy.

31...♕c8 32 ♗xc6 ♕xc6 33 a6 ♔g7 34 ♖b4 ♘d6 35 ♕a4 ♕xa4 36 ♖xa4 ♘c8

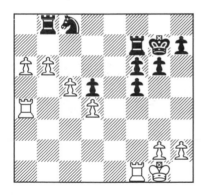

The knight won't help Black. Note that Topalov failed to make anything of his extra kingside pawns which, to be fair, lacked the harmony of White's on the queenside.

37 ♖b4!

37 ♖b1 would be careless in view of

37...♘a7, when the b-pawn is pinned to a rook that can be captured with check. This is not the case after ♖b4.

37...♘a7

37...♔f8 38 ♖a1 wins for White.

38 bxa7 ♖a8 39 c6 ♖axa7

39...♖fxa7 40 ♖b7+.

40 ♖c1 1-0

The next game almost made it into the Miniatures chapter but, apart from being a move over the limit, it is an instructive example of how quickly we can find our structure falling apart – and how quickly this can then lead to throwing in the towel.

Spassky-Avtonomov
Leningrad 1949

1 d4 d5 2 c4 dxc4 3 ♘f3 ♘f6 4 e3 c5 5 ♗xc4 e6 6 0-0 a6 7 ♕e2 b5 8 ♗b3

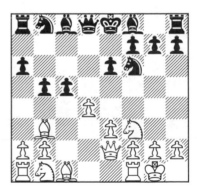

Now Black should play 8...♗b7, after which the queen's knight tends to find itself on d7. Then a sample line is (8...♗b7) 9 a4 ♘bd7 10 axb5 axb5 11 ♖xa8 ♕xa8 and for the moment ♕xb5 is not on.

8...♘c6?!

An inaccuracy that White fails to punish.

9 ♘c3?!

White returns the favour. After seeing 8...♗b7 9 a4 it is clear that the line 9 a4 is appropriate here as 9...♗b7? simply loses a pawn to 10 axb5 axb5 11 ♖xa8 ♕xa8 12 ♕xb5 etc. Black's best is 9...c4, when 10 ♗c2 ♗b7 11 axb5 axb5 12 ♖xa8 ♗xa8 13 ♘c3 is much easier to play for White, e.g. 13...♕b6 14 b3 cxb3 15 ♗xb3 with an advantage in the form of the b-pawn (a target), the potentially mobile centre and a lead in development.

9...cxd4?

Presumably part of Black's plan. By-passing the d-pawn and trying to keep the position closed with 9...c4 10 ♗c2 might be best, although the option of a timely a2-a4 and the 2–1 pawn advantage in the centre should favour White. But this looks preferable for Black to 9...b4 10 ♘a4, which in turn looks better than the text.

10 ♖d1

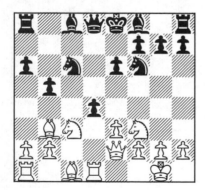

A standard theme in this opening, forcing the return of the pawn. Now Black could choose to surrender it with 10...d3, borrowing an idea from an-other, quite similar line. At least then White can try for an advantage only with e3-e4, while the rook might have to waste a tempo by retreating to d1.

10...♗b7

Again Black has a specific idea in mind, but a change of direction was necessary here, with 10...♗e7 followed by castling being by far the most appropriate continuation. Ironically, the whole point of Black's approach is based on an oversight, albeit one which most players would fail to spot...

11 exd4 ♘b4

By now 11...♗e7 invites White to break open the centre with 12 d5, when 12...exd5 13 ♘xd5 ♘xd5 14 ♗xd5 seems to put Black in trouble wherever the queen runs to, e.g. 14...♕c7 15 ♕e4 ♖c8 (15...♘d8 16 ♗f4 ♗xd5 17 ♖xd5 ♕a7 18 ♖ad1) 16 ♗f4 ♕b6 17 ♖e1 etc. Of course after the text Black need no longer worry about d4-d5 and will therefore be able to complete development.

12 d5!

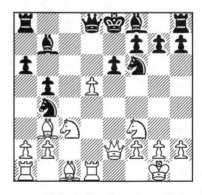

Remember – it is always worth checking over a move or idea that you would like to make even if it seems unlikely, just in case it is actually playable. In this case Black engineered a situation in which he concentrated exclusively on the d5-square (two knights, queen, bishop and pawn) in order to rule out any funny business with d4-d5, yet White can push anyway. Often when this happens the 'prevented' move or plan turns out to be as dangerous – or more so – than was originally feared, probably because the pieces used to nip it in the bud neglect other (now important) duties in doing so.

12...♘bxd5 13 ♗g5!

Effectively creating a third pin, this aggressive move is really what makes the gambit. Black has no choice but to allow serious damage to his kingside pawn structure.

13...♗e7

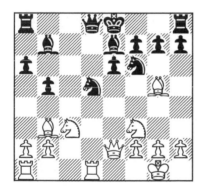

14 ♗xf6! gxf6

Forced in view of the pinned e-pawn after ....♗xf6. Unfortunately for Black his control of d5 has just gone down a notch, so the cluster of three pawns is about to break up, ruining the pawn structure altogether.

15 ♘xd5 ♗xd5

15...exd5 keeps a would-be defender on the board but this does not help Black: 16 ♘d4 ♗c8 (16...0-0? 17 ♘f5

threatens the bishop as well as mate in two) 17 ♘c6 ♕d6 18 ♗xd5 and White is winning.

16 ♗xd5 exd5 17 ♘d4

Black is practically losing and he can thank his terrible pawn structure for the predicament. Castling is out of the question as (17...0-0) 18 ♘f5 forks e7 as well as (with ♕g4+) g7. Note that White's gambit was aimed at reaching this very position – which is great – so there would be no point in merely winning back the sacrificed pawn with 17 ♕d2. Instead White prefers to highlight his opponent's weaknesses as quickly as possible before Black has an opportunity to consolidate.

17...♔f8

Escaping the pin. Perhaps a lesser evil is to first offer protection along the rank: 17...♕d7 18 ♖e1 ♖a7 19 ♖ac1 and White threatens 20 ♕xe7+! ♕xe7 21 ♖c8+ ♔d7 22 ♖xe7+ etc. Consequently 19...♔f8 is forced, after which 20 ♕h5 (followed by ♘f5 or the immediate check on h6) should wrap up the full point sooner rather than later.

18 ♘f5

Next comes ♕h5-h6+, hence Black's response.

18...h5

18...♗c5 removes the bishop from one firing line but places it in another after 19 ♖ac1, e.g. 19...♖c8 (19...♕b6 20 ♖xd5) 20 b4! ♕d7 (20...♗xb4 21 ♖xc8 ♕xc8 22 ♕g4) 21 ♕f3 ♗b6 22 ♕xd5! etc. Meanwhile, 18...♖a7 loses to 19 ♕e3!, with a big threat on each flank.

19 ♖xd5!

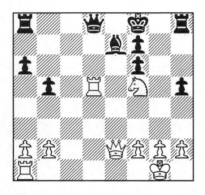

19...♕xd5

Tantamount to resignation, although the line 19...♕c7 20 ♖ad1 is depressing (20...♖d8 21 ♕xe7+!) and 19...♕e8 20 ♕d2 followed by ♖e1 will not alter the eventual result.

20 ♕xe7+ ♔g8 21 ♕xf6 1-0

After allowing d4-d5 in the first place (and how many club players saw that coming after Black's d5-themed play?), Black had insufficient control of the game, which disappeared over the horizon at a fair speed of knots.

Note that the general course of this game was in stark contrast to Bronstein's gambit. There White's play revolved around a gradual exploitation of Black's damaged pawns which culminated in a decisive endgame advantage, whereas in this example Black's poor structure simply led to him being unable to adequately defend straight out of the opening.

CHAPTER SEVEN

Miniatures

Here is a collection of gambit miniatures that attracted my attention while researching for the book. The common denominator is the loser's inability to cope with the gambit situation (even if he helped create it).

Abonyi-Hromadka
Prague 1908

1 e4 e5 2 ♘f3 ♘c6 3 ♘c3

Black teasingly throws in ...♘d4 in this game, but here is an even more audacious example: 3 ♗c4 ♘d4?!

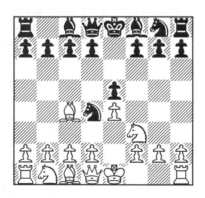

After answering 1 e4 with 1...e5 and then being faced with a fairly aggressive opening, Black immediately moves his only developed piece for the second time and offers the e5-pawn, the capture of which will leave the traditional weak spot f7 under fire. *NCO* gives the sober 4 ♘xd4 exd4 5 0-0 with a clear lead for White, who is well ahead in development, but let us see what happens if White accepts the gambit: 4 ♘xe5? ♕g5! (the point – Black happily invites either capture on f7...) 5 ♘xf7 ♕xg2 6 ♖f1 (6 ♘xh8 loses after 6...♕xh1+ 7 ♗f1 ♕xe4+ 8 ♗e2 ♘xc2+, when White must part with the queen in view of 9 ♔f1 ♕h1 mate) 6...♕xe4+ 7 ♗e2 ♘f3 mate

This would be nice. White's fun also comes to a sticky end after 5 ♗xf7+ ♔d8, e.g. 6 ♗xg8 ♕xg2 7 ♖f1 ♕xe4+ etc. I wouldn't recommend 3...♘d4 against sensible players but if you don't mind lagging behind in development (after 4 ♘xd4) you might meet the occasional taker...

3...♘f6 4 ♗b5 ♘d4

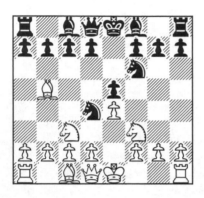

Again Black is prepared at such an early stage of the opening to both move a piece for the second time and surrender the e5-pawn. It is this proposed gambit, of course, upon which the course of the game is decided, depending on how White addresses the offer.

5 ♗a4

For the moment White is more interested in preserving his bishop than grabbing the pawn. 5 ♘xe5 ♕e7 6 f4 ♘xb5 7 ♘xb5 d6 8 ♘f3 ♕xe4+ is equal. Neishtadt writes in *Winning Quickly with Black* that 'the attempt by 9 ♔f2 to exploit the e-file costs White dearly...' (9 ♕e2 ♕xe2+ 10 ♔xe2 ♘d5 looks a shade better for Black if anyone) with the following lines: 9...♘g4+ 10 ♔g3 (10 ♔g1 ♕c6 11 ♕e2+ ♗e7 12 h3 ♕b6+ 13 d4 ♘f6 is not clear) 10...♕g6 11 ♘h4 ♕h5 12 ♘xc7+? (12 h3 ♕xb5

13 hxg4 g5!) 12...♔d8 13 h3 (White might be able to get away with 13 ♘xa8, e.g. 13...g5 14 fxg5 d5 15 d3 ♗d6+ 16 ♗f4 ♕xg5 17 ♕f3 ♘f6+ 18 ♔f2 ♗xf4 19 g3 ♗e3+ 20 ♔g2 ♗g4 21 ♕f1) 13...♘f6 14 ♘xa8 ♕xh4+ 15 ♔xh4 ♘e4

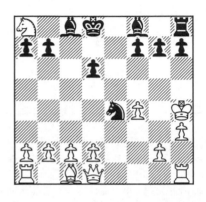

... 'and wins' in view of the threat of mate with ...♗e7 etc. However, Black has invested so much material in his quest to catch the king that White currently has a queen and a rook for a bishop(!), so it is worth seeing how the game might continue after 16 ♕h5 (or the cheeky 16 ♕g4!?) 16...♗e7+ 17 ♕g5 ♗xg5+ 18 fxg5 h6 19 g6 fxg6. Now mate looms, with 20 g4?, for example, running into 20...♗d7! and the bishop will deliver mate on e8. It seems that 20 ♖f1! is forced, when there can follow 20...g5+ (20...♗d7 21 ♖f7 g5+ 22 ♔h5 ♗e8 23 ♔g6 ♖f8 24 d3 ♘f6 25 ♔xg7 ♖xf7+ 26 ♔xh6 sees White emerge with a collection of pawns to compensate for the fall of the knight) 21 ♔h5 ♘g3+ 22 ♔g6 ♘xf1 23 ♔xg7 ♖e8 24 d3 ♗e6 25 ♗xg5+ hxg5 26 ♖xf1 ♖g8+ and Black should be in front, e.g. 27 ♔h7 ♔d7 28 ♖f5 ♖xa8 29 ♖xg5 ♗xa2, or 27 ♔f6 ♖f8+ 28 ♔xe6 ♖xf1 29 ♔xd6 ♖f6+ etc.

That was rather complicated and definitely needs testing, but serves as an excellent warning not to end your opening preparation on the 8th move!

5 ♘xd4 exd4 6 e5 dxc3 7 exf6 is temporarily interesting and even clearly better for White if Black accepts the gambit pawn with 7...cxd2+ 8 ♗xd2 ♕xf6 9 0-0, when Black is miles behind in development – his queen, traditionally, being the only piece to see daylight. In fact a good demonstration of how events can so quickly reach decisive levels can be seen if Black accepts the second pawn: 9...♕xb2 10 ♖e1+ ♗e7 11 ♖b1

Black is deservedly punished, as ♗b4 is coming, when the d-pawn is pinned. Alternatively, 10...♔d8 is a big improvement but looks awful after, say, 11 ♕h5. However, the safe 7...♕xf6 8 dxc3 ♕e5+ leads to equality, many games seeing the peaceful 9 ♕e2 ♕xe2+ 10 ♗xe2 d5 as tantamount to a draw.

5...c6

The other main move is 5...♗c5, when after 6 ♘xe5 0-0 7 ♘d3 ♗b6 8 e5 ♘e8 White tends to avoid 9 0-0 d6 10 exd6 ♘f6!? and opts instead for a relocation with 9 ♘d5 d6 10 ♘e3, when

NCO gives 10...c5 11 c3 ♘f5 12 exd6 ♕xd6 13 ♗c2 ♘f6 14 0-0 ♗c7 15 g3, and Black's compensation for the gambit pawn is obvious.

6 0-0

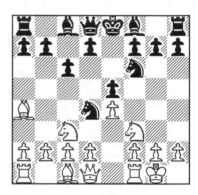

This time White puts the safety of his king ahead of material considerations, but the carrot still dangles in front of him after Black's reply... 6 ♘xe5 d5! 7 0-0 ♕d6 8 f4 b5 9 ♗b3 was seen in Short-Piket, Debrecen 1992, while NCO gives 7 d3 ♗d6 8 f4 0-0 9 0-0 b5 10 ♗b3 b4 as equal.

6...♗c5?!

6...b5 7 ♗b3 a5 8 ♘xe5 ♕e7 9 ♘d3 a4 10 e5 axb3 11 exf6 ♕xf6 12 cxb3 ♗e7 offers chances for both sides according to Neishtadt. NCO gives 6...♕a5! 7 ♖e1 d6 8 h3 ♗e7 9 a3 0-0 10 b4 ♕c7 as equal.

7 ♘xe5

An interesting psychological decision from White, who could have continued to hold firm and ignore the e5-pawn with the solid 7 d3. However, it always feels safer to accept such a gambit when you have a few pieces in play and you've given your king a safe haven after castling – particularly with the white pieces and a slight development advantage!

7...d6 8 ♘d3!

Avoiding the pin in view of the difficulties White might experience after 8 ♘f3 ♗g4 9 d3 ♕d7, e.g. 10 ♗e3 ♗xf3 11 gxf3 ♕h3 12 ♗xd4 ♗xd4 13 ♘e2 ♗e5 14 ♘g3 (14 f4 ♘g4 mates) 14...h5 and Black is having all the fun.

8...♗g4 9 ♕e1 ♘f3+?

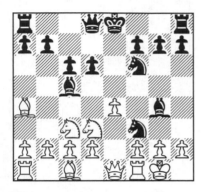

The trouble with gambits is that when they fail to deliver the desired scenario we are behind on points. However, Black takes the bull by the horns and elects to test his opponent's nerve...

10 gxf3 ♗xf3 11 e5 0-0

Black's only hope is White's lonely king and White's ability to deal with the unusual situation.

12 exd6?

I was going to award 12 ♘xc5 with an exclamation mark but it is actually rather obvious. Perhaps White was not happy with the position after 12...♕c8 13 e6 dxc5, when the threat of ...b7-b5 puts him on the defensive on both flanks. However, White is a piece up, and with 14 ♕e3 can emerge from the storm with a clear lead. Unfortunately for White, the text aims to take the sting out of Black's attack with an exchange of queens.

12...♘g4

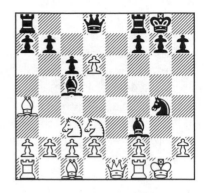

13 ♕e7??

According to plan, and losing. Absolutely necessary is 13 ♘e5, when 13...♘xh2 14 d4 ♗xd6 15 ♕e3 ♕h4 16 ♕f4 ♕xf4 17 ♗xf4 ♘xf1 18 ♔xf1 should favour the minor pieces, but 13...♖e8 14 ♘xf3 ♖xe1 15 ♘xe1 ♕xd6 still looks good for Black – despite White's collection of pieces for the queen – in view of the continued pressure on White's king. At least the game continues, though, which is not the case after ♕e7.

13...♗xd6! 0-1

Black deserves some credit for his consistency and positive approach here, the decisive threatened mate on h2 a fitting end to a game that saw the systematic dismantling of White's defences. Perhaps I have been too critical of White's poor/mistaken resistance as it can be rather disconcerting to come under attack so early in the game – that's what gambit play is all about.

In the following game White's busy queen accounts for more than a third of his total moves and, ironically, ends a journey that reaches into enemy territory by being closed out of the game on b1.

Astfalk-Mellerowicz
Oranienbaum 1989

1 d4 d5 2 c4 e6 3 ♘c3 c5 4 cxd5 cxd4

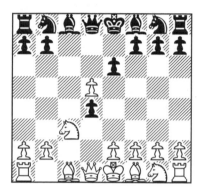

The fiery Hennig-Schara is a no-nonsense gambit designed to accelerate Black's development. With correct play White should secure an advantage, albeit in complex positions that require a good nerve and careful handling, typically with the kings being sent to opposite flanks. Not surprisingly this is fairly popular at club level. If White is insufficiently acquainted with the gambit he can quickly run into trouble.

5 ♕xd4

Throwing in 5 ♕a4+ introduces the main line, which goes 5...♗d7 6 ♕xd4 exd5 7 ♕xd5 ♘c6 8 ♘f3 ♘f6 9 ♕d1 (9 ♕b3 ♗e6) 9...♗c5 10 e3 ♕e7 11 ♗e2 0-0-0 12 0-0 g5

See following diagram

If you like gambits then this could be your cup of tea, while I am sure that the diagram position looks quite intimidat-

ing if you don't like facing gambits.

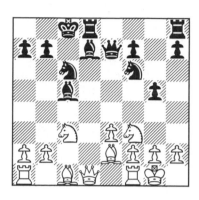

The safer option is to favour 3 ♘f3 over 3 ♘c3. Otherwise, a key theme in this tense situation, with the g-pawn charging down the board, is to serve up some of the same with b2-b4 and, since Black rather cheekily forgot to prepare ...g7-g5, the recommended reaction here is 13 b4. Anyway, my point is that this line certainly gives Black value, and it is worth investigating further if you're looking for ideas against 1 d4.

5...♘c6

At the earliest opportunity Black takes advantage of his opponent's exposed queen, developing for free.

6 ♕d1 exd5 7 ♕xd5

The d5-pawn is an offer that cannot be realistically refused in view of Black's space and free and easy development. 7 ♘xd5 helps Black after, say, 7...♘f6.

7...♗e6

As we can see from the next note, Black's development lead is such that a trade of queens will not diminish the coming initiative. However, from a psychological perspective, the diagram position is far from easy for White to handle if he is not well versed with the theory. Exchanging queens might seem illogical because not only would that surrender a piece that has already moved three times for one that has not moved at all, but the recapture brings the rook into play. White's next, on the other hand, keeps the queen busy and takes aim at a second pawn.

8 ♕b5?

Better is 8 ♕xd8+ ♖xd8 9 e3, when Black should seek to exploit his lead in development with a quick offensive: 9...♘b4 10 ♗b5+ ♔e7 11 ♔f1 g5!?

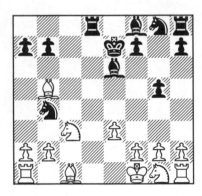

I'm not sure that Black's compensation is worth a full pawn in this odd position, which is why it has been evaluated as slightly favourable for White. Nevertheless, knowledge is power, and if White is making it up for

himself in this variation (by no means a certainty, as this game demonstrates) I would prefer to be sitting on Black's side of the board.

8...a6 9 ♕xb7 ♘b4

With the juicy threat of mate in one.

10 ♕e4 ♘f6 11 ♕b1 ♗c8

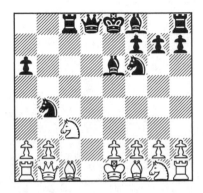

Black's gambit has now doubled to two pawns, in return for which he has been allowed to generate a dangerous attack.

12 a3

Asked to suggest a move in the position after 11...♗c8, many players would initially be drawn to the text, seeking to evict Black's most advanced and annoying piece. 12 e3 is an alternative but White might have been put off by 12...♗c4 or quite simply considered only a retreat of the attacked knight. However, a look at White's kingside suggests that the king could be stuck in the centre longer than is healthy, while Black will soon mobilise the rest of his forces. Consequently, at least in practical terms, two pawns seems like a fair price to pay to put White under pressure. The investment certainly brings dividends in the game.

12...♗b3!

Easy to appreciate, easy to overlook. White might have been regretting his strategy at this point.

13 axb4 ♖xc3!

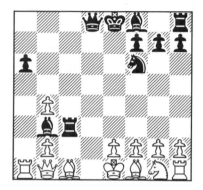

Very nice, and illustrating once again a key theme of this book. In today's 'educated' chess world gambit play might be considerably more positionally oriented than in the coffee house era but, essentially, success will only come with the help of what is effectively an optimistic, aggressive, open-to-sacrificial-possibilities attitude. In this game Black's gambit play works because he is thinking along the lines of a quick strike. Hopefully the diagram position will serve as a warning to juniors who think nothing of sending the queen around the board in search of random threats and unprotected pawns. White's only 'in play' piece has just been removed, the queen looks quite comical and the rest of the forces have not even been touched.

14 ♗d2

No prizes for seeing 14 bxc3 ♕d1 mate.

See following diagram

However, I couldn't resist the urge to garnish the mate with a tasty dessert of a diagram, for in the dozen or so chess books that I have written over the years this is one of the oddest final positions and thus merits the extra ink. Evidence suggests that White has had development problems.

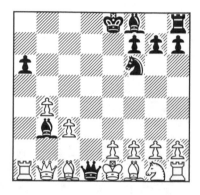

14...♖c2 15 ♘f3 ♘e4 16 ♗c3 ♗xb4! 0-1

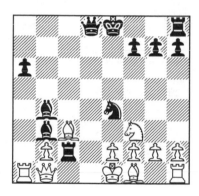

A nice piece of geometry with which to prompt White's resignation. The point is that 17 ♗xb4 ♕b6 hits b4 and f2.

The Slav Defence has an undeserved reputation for being solid. Perhaps this is because White has the option of trying to kill off the game with the symmetrical Exchange Variation. In our next miniature Black's energetic gambit play, helped by White's early development of the queen, catches the enemy king in the centre.

Cserna-Szollosi
Hungary 1983

1 d4 d5 2 c4 c6 3 ♘f3 ♘f6 4 ♕c2 ♘a6 5 ♗f4

In hindsight it might be better to settle for the modest 5 e3.

5...♘b4 6 ♕b3 e5

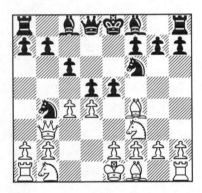

Ooh! Black is intent on fighting for the initiative after being given the opportunity to quickly infiltrate with his knight, and he is willing to gambit a pawn to achieve this.

7 dxe5

White has three ways to accept the gambit, and Black is able to generate sufficient activity in each scenario. After 7 ♗xe5 dxc4 8 ♕xc4 (8 ♕d1 ♗f5) 8...♗e6 followed by ...♘xa2 White is under fire but has no pawn to show for his troubles, while 7 ♘xe5 dxc4 8 ♕xc4 ♗e6 or 8 ♘xc4 ♕xd4 9 e3 ♕d8 also very much favour Black. By capturing with the d-pawn White hopes to at least

see Black inconvenienced by the tension in the centre.

7...♗f5 8 ♘a3

Not 8 exf6 because after 8...♘c2+ 9 ♔d1 Black has 9...dxc4+.

8...♘e4

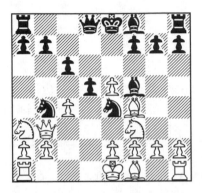

The second knight jumps in. Black's advantages in the diagram position are not immediately evident, so I have some sympathy for White in the way he found himself in difficulties after just a few moves. In fact Black's gambit is easy to underestimate – or even miss – at the board. Anyway, as we delve further into this position, the extent of White's defensive task is quite surprising considering the fact that he is still ahead in development. The main problem is the kingside, the development of which has suffered at the cost of the queenside pieces. Consequently White's king must remain in the centre. Meanwhile, his pieces are not particularly well posted, the most obvious being the a3-knight, misplaced thanks to the threatened check on c2. The queen also makes matters worse for White after Black's latest because ...♘c5 could prove quite awkward. For example White really needs to usher his king to safety but the move that he wants to play, 9 e3, is punished by 9...♘c5!, the idea being that ♕xb4 loses the queen to ...♘d3+ etc. This leaves 10 ♕c3 or 10 ♕d1, when in both cases Black can hold back on the strong check on d3 and first turn the screw further with 10...♕a5.

9 cxd5

Adding another pawn to the collection. 9 ♘d4 is an attempt at active defence, and again Black has the aggressive 9...♕a5!

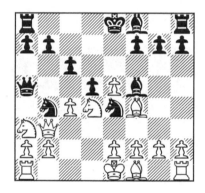

The threats on the e1–a5 diagonal highlight White's dilemma. Unfortunately (for White) 10 0-0-0 ♘c5 hits the queen, which now prevents mate on a2, while after 10 ♘xf5 ♘c2+ 11 ♔d1 ♘xa1 12 ♕xb7 ♘xf2+ Black won't be picking up the second rook in view of the mate on e1. 9 ♘d2 is a typical exchanging defensive resource but Black emerges well on top after either 9...♘xd2 10 ♗xd2 dxc4, e.g. 11 ♕xc4 ♗e6 and ...♘xa2, or 9...♗c5 10 ♘xe4 dxe4 11 e3 ♕a5 (11...0-0) 12 0-0-0 0-0

See following diagram

White's king is not ready to relax in view of a timely ...b7-b5. Looking at

these lines, and many others throughout this book, we are too busy dealing with the array of interesting options made possible by the initial gambit to actually care about the defender's modest material lead.

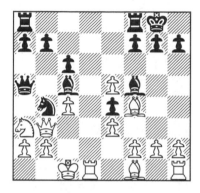

9...♗c5

9...♘xd5 10 ♗d2 ♗c5 11 e3 ♕e7 is also good but Black is closing in for the kill...

10 ♗e3

The alternative is 10 e3, when Black has two choices. After 10...♘xd5 11 ♗c4 ♗b4+ 12 ♔f1 Black has obvious compensation for the pawn, but more interesting is the thematic 10...♕a5 11 ♘c4

The queen is attacked but there are

checks on d3 and c2, each producing quite different results. Black emerges ahead on points after 11...♘c2+ 12 ♔e2 ♘xa1 13 ♘xa5 ♘xb3 14 ♘xb3 cxd5, while it is possible to keep the gambit fire burning with 11...♘d3+ 12 ♔e2 ♘xf4+ 13 exf4 ♕a6

White's king continues to be harassed and he will miss the dark-squared bishop, but the centre pawns offer him something, and the struggle goes on.

10...♕a5

The key move, as we have seen.

11 ♘d2

This time 11 ♘c4 backfires completely: 11...♘c2+ 12 ♔d1 ♗xe3!

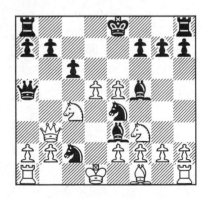

A strange position. After only a dozen moves Black has more pieces in

control of the squares around White's king than his opponent, culminating in the delivery of a brutal looking mate on f2 after ♘xa5. Either recapture of the bishop will see the fall of a rook or two.

11...♗xe3 12 ♕xe3 ♘xd5?!

Natural but Black misses 12...♕xa3! with a couple of forks to follow, e.g. 13 ♕xa3 ♘c2+ 14 ♔d1 ♘xf2+ etc. Here 13 ♕xe4 ♕xb2 sees Black win material.

13 ♕d4

13 ♕d3 ♘xf2 14 ♕xf5 ♘xh1 might be a lesser evil, although White is on the ropes there, too.

13...♘b4 0-1

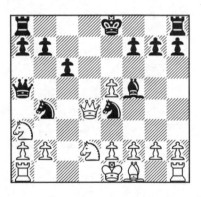

White resigned in view of the threat 14...♕xa3 15 bxa3 ♘c2+ and 16...♘xd4 etc. 14 ♘xe4 ♘c2+ is out of the question, 14 ♕e3 ♖d8 is final and 14 e6 merely postpones the end after 14...♖d8 15 exf7+ ♔xf7 16 ♕c4+ ♖d5 etc.

The Albin Counter-Gambit is rarely seen above a certain level in international practice because White is able to engineer a comfortable advantage in more than one fashion. Of course a certain amount of theoretical knowledge and skill is required to achieve this, which explains why the uncompromising answer to the Queen's Gambit is fairly popular with club players (who also like to have a bit of entertainment and value for money when they sit down to play with the black pieces).

Gil-Leontxo Garcia
Benidorm 1983

1 d4 d5 2 c4 e5

Black ignores the gambit c4-pawn and makes an offer of his own. This gambit is designed to facilitate rapid piece play by opening lines in the centre and, with the coming advance of the d-pawn, create an early space advantage in order to hinder White's development. Theoretically suspect it may be, but if White does not tread carefully it could soon be time to go home.

3 dxe5

Incidentally, 3 cxd5 ♕xd5 4 e3 exd4 5 exd4 ♘c6 6 ♘f3 ♗g4 leads to a line of the Scotch Gambit that White does best to avoid.

3...d4 4 ♘f3

4 e3? challenges the new arrival and does not seem like a poor move, but it is. In fact life can get much worse:

4...♗b4+! 5 ♗d2 dxe3!

The point of this capture is to meet 6 ♗xb4?? exf2+ 7 ♔e2 with 7...fxg1♘+!

Aha! The automatic promotion to a queen should be roughly level after 8 ♕xd8+ and 9 ♖xg1, but the check is decisive because now 8 ♖xg1 allows 8...♗g4+ etc. Instead there can follow 8 ♔e1 ♕h4+ 9 ♔d2 (9 g3 ♕e4+) 9...♘c6 10 ♗c3 ♗g4 and Black is about to castle long with check and close the deal. It is this trap that has been responsible for attracting so many to the Albin Counter-Gambit. Regardless of how many times it appears in print there will always be enough victims, and how many other openings offer you an opportunity to underpromote — with check – on the seventh move?

Returning to the position after 5...dxe3!, White can try 6 ♕a4+ ♘c6 7 ♗xb4 exf2+ 8 ♔xf2. Then Linse-Kjelberg, Malmo 1917 continued 8...♕h4+ 9 ♔e3 ♕d4+ 10 ♔f3 ♗g4+ 11 ♔g3 ♘h6 12 h3 ♘f5+ 13 ♔h2 ♕f4+

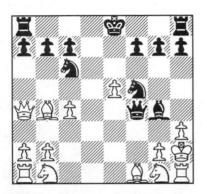

White is deservedly punished for neglecting the kingside. If this miniature were not enough, what about Petrov-Panteleev, Bulgaria 1973, which saw White block the check with 9 g3, when 9...♕d4+ 10 ♔g2 ♕xb2+ 11 ♘d2 ♕xa1 12 ♘gf3 ♕b2 13 a3 ♗g4 0-1 was another 'unlucky' 13-mover for White

Best is 6 fxe3, e.g. 6...♕h4+ 7 g3 ♕e4 8 ♕f3 ♗xd2+ 9 ♘xd2 ♕xe5 10 0-0-0 ♘f6 with chances for both sides, although there is room for improvement for Black here. Anyway, 4 ♘f3 avoids all this pain.

4...♘c6 5 g3

I like 5 ♘bd2, dispensing with the kingside fianchetto in favour of queenside expansion with a2-a3 and b2-b4, as well as introducing the idea of rounding up the d4-pawn with ♘b3.

5...♗g4 6 ♗g2 ♕d7 7 0-0 0-0-0 8 ♕b3

In good old gambit tradition we find

ourselves with the kings on opposite flanks. White's latest is a dual-purpose move, the queen teaming up with the light-squared bishop to exert pressure on the b7-pawn, as well as vacating d1 for the rook to hit d4. Consequently Black must be consistent and seek to keep White busy on the kingside.

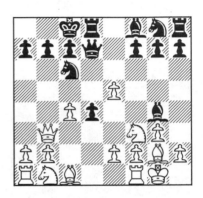

8...h5

Black wastes no time, although this is not best. However, it is a definite improvement on the natural 8...♗h3? in view of the strong counter 9 e6!, when Black is in trouble because the sudden break in communication fits in with White's set-up. 9...♕xe6 loses to 10 ♘g5, so forced is 9...♗xe6, when things start to get ugly thanks to 10 ♘e5

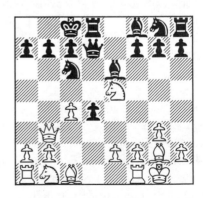

With a timely counter-gambit(!) White's clearance of the e5-square for the knight helps unleash the bishop and bring the queen into play. Since ...♘xe5 permits immediate mate, Black has no choice but to accept serious structural damage in front of his king after 10...♕d6 11 ♘xc6 bxc6, when he can forget the kingside attack. This is a good illustration of how the product of a gambit (Black's attacking prospects) can suddenly disappear if the opposition is given the chance to engineer an effective counter-gambit. A decent alternative to the thrust of the h-pawn is 8...♕f5, e.g. 9 ♖d1 ♘ge7 10 ♘a3 ♘g6 11 ♘c2 ♗c5 12 ♘ce1 ♗b6 13 ♘d3 (that was quite a manoeuvre) 13...♗xf3 14 ♗xf3 ♘cxe5 15 ♗g2 with an edge for White in Budnikov-Meszaros, Lenk 1993. Black's forces are reasonably well placed and he has picked up the e5-pawn along the way but, significantly, the g2-bishop will take some watching.

9 ♘bd2?

In this kind of situation, with pieces and pawns taking aim at the kings, time is of paramount importance. The active follow-up to ♕b3 is 9 ♖d1 with the immediate threat of ♘xd4!, again exploiting the vulnerability of the b7-pawn. However, if White is unaware of this theme, then ♖d1 might seem slow, which just goes to show how the course of the game can take any direction in such complex situations. As we should now be aware, whether a gambit is sound is not necessarily as relevant a factor as what impact it might have on both the game and the opposition.

9...h4

In gambit mode, Black needs no guidance as to finding a plan – simply open the h-file and keep the focus of attention on White's king.

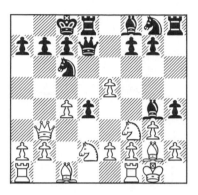

10 ♘xh4

In view of what happens perhaps the ugly 10 gxh4 is necessary, ugly being the appropriate word.

10...♗xe2 11 ♖e1 d3

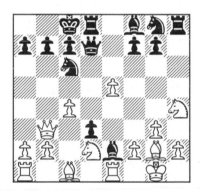

Matters have taken a downward turn for White, who now finds the mutually defended bishop and passed pawn a little too close for comfort. The h-file is a cause for concern, White has lost touch with the d4-square and the e5-pawn (for the moment the knight must remain on c6), and the g1–a7 diagonal is waiting for Black's bishop to take up residence.

12 ♘hf3 ♕f5

Tying White down to the defence of the knight and stepping closer to the enemy king.

13 ♕b5 a6 14 ♕a4 ♘xe5

Here it comes...

15 ♘xe5 ♕xf2+! 0-1

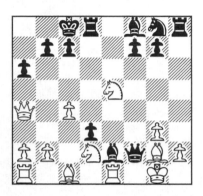

The power of the two bishops is demonstrated after 16 ♔xf2 ♗c5 mate.

White's unfortunate treatment of the opening led to his demise. Black also went astray but, as he selected the playing field with 2...e5, he is clearly at home playing gambits and was soon able to focus. Quite possibly, a more sober opening such as the Exchange Variation of the Queen's Gambit, with its characteristic structure and strategies, would have suited White, but this game was played on Black's territory.

To be fair to Black in the next game he employs a variation of the Sicilian Defence that features an early entry into the game of the queen. In such circumstances, of course, extra care is required. Add to this the fact that the opposition's name is Tal, and being on the wrong side of a miniature could be on the cards.

Tal-Hamann

Kizlovodsk 1966

1 e4 c5 2 ♘f3 e6 3 d4 cxd4 4 ♘xd4 a6 5 ♘c3 ♕c7

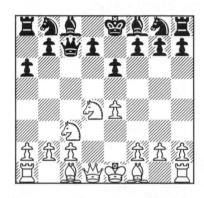

The Kan system (4...a6) is an intriguing animal in that Black tends to hold back his minor pieces temporarily until he sees what set-up White chooses. This might seem rather risky when we consider the often cut-throat nature of the Open Sicilian but, as if to emphasise the point, Black's flexibility is demonstrated by the fact that the first piece to come out is the queen (from c7 the queen monitors some potentially important squares, with the c-file and the b8-h2 diagonal providing Black with numerous options as the game progresses). Depending on White's chosen configuration, Black will develop accordingly; even I have toyed with the Kan (briefly, and poorly timed – against strong, experienced opposition). An occupational hazard is that when things go wrong they can do so quite dramatically.

6 ♗e2 ♘f6

6...b5 is a Kan theme.

7 0-0 ♗b4

7...♘c6 steers the game into the

calmer waters of the Taimanov.

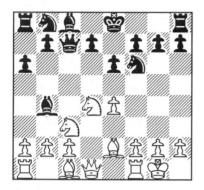

8 ♗g5

8 ♕d3 is the alternative, when 8...♘c6 9 ♗g5 ♘e5 10 ♕g3 gives the game a different flavour.

8...♗xc3 9 ♗xf6!

The point, and typical Tal, who was never one to hesitate when it came to creating complications. Notice that any kind of disruption or increase in the game's temperature has a good chance of working for White thanks to his already considerable lead in development. Consequently we don't need Tal's genius to appreciate that such a destabilisation is perfect gambit material.

9...gxf6

Black has a plan, and the alternative

further clearing of the long diagonal is excellent for White after 9...♗xb2 10 ♗xg7 ♗xa1 11 ♗xh8 ♗c3 12 ♕d3!

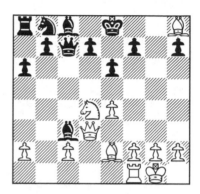

Material is level but White threatens ♘xe6 followed by ♗xc3, while e4-e5 will simply take complete control of the kingside (surrendering the bishop for knight here leaves White in charge of the dark squares).

10 bxc3

Both sides have doubled pawns but the significant difference is that Black's damage is in front of his king (castling short is clearly out of the question).

10...♕xc3?!

10...♕f4 moves the queen for a second time when it seems that Black has more constructive things to do, but this is a Kan type idea and is preferable to the greedy text. Perhaps best is 10...♘c6, challenging the well posted knight and seeking to alleviate some of the pressure. Hamann accepts the offer, but is it worth the time, given that he has structural problems and no other pieces in play? England's wise GM Keith Arkell asks in this kind of situation whether Black would invest what is – particularly in the opening phase of the game – a valuable tempo in placing the queen on c3 if the square were not occupied by a pawn. I recommend that you ask yourself this question when contemplating such pawn captures. In this case, playing ...♕c3 rather than ...♕xc3 would be ridiculous.

11 ♖b1

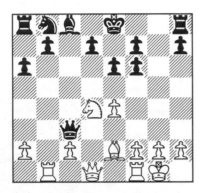

A nice move. White has more in mind than just eyeing the b7-pawn. Instead the newly arrived queen is to be used to gain yet more time.

11...♘c6 12 ♘xc6 dxc6?

Opening the d-file is as wrong as it looks. Black must adhere to the 'capture towards the centre' rule, when at least a defensive wall of five pawns offers the king some kind of shelter after 12...bxc6 13 ♖b3 ♕c5 14 ♔h1

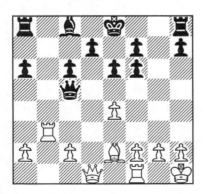

White is ready to add the f-pawn to his attacking force, which already numbers enough pieces to maintain the pressure. Black will have problems doing anything other than consolidating; it is difficult to see how the bishop can get into the game (although it serves a purpose protecting d7) and subsequently whether the rooks will get acquainted, while the queen can only help hold the position together. White has targets in d7, d6, f6 and g7 and has the b-file to himself, while Black cannot really afford to lose either of the rook's pawns because White's resulting passed pawn might prove problematic. Some players don't mind defending Black's position if it means being in possession of the gambit pawn, while others prefer White's control and targets. However, these positions tend to be easier for the side in 'control' as the significance of the pawn could take a while in coming.

13 ♖b3 ♕c5 14 ♕d2

This is the kind of position that makes us wonder why we don't happily gambit pawns at every opportunity (after due consideration, of course). If presented with the position, would you count up the pawns and come to the conclusion that Black is better? Or would you scan the board to see White's lead in development, active pieces and the contrasting king positions and opt to step into White's shoes? My guess is the latter – otherwise you need to lighten up a little. Counting pawns can be a bad habit. It is just as important (and useful) to count weak squares, vulnerable pawns, good pieces, poor pieces and other factors that combine to create a position. Apart from vacating d1 for the king's rook, the text also threatens to send the queen up to h6, which would highlight the weaknesses around the black king. This is a serious enough incursion to justify Black's next.

14...h5 15 ♖d1! ♔e7

15...♔f8 16 ♕d8+ ♔g7 17 ♖g3+ puts the rook's location on the third rank – facilitated by Black's acceptance of the gambit – to decisive use. 15...♕e7 16 ♖d3 won't help Black: 16...♔f8 (16...0-0 17 ♕h6) 17 ♖d8+ ♔g7 18 ♖xh8 ♔xh8 19 ♕h6+ ♔g8 20 ♖d3 h4 21 ♕xh4 etc.

16 ♖d3 ♕b6

16...♕g5 abandons the queenside and invites 17 ♕b4+ c5 18 ♕b6.

17 e5! 1-0

Black cannot allow the deadly 18 exf6+, while 17...fxe5 18 ♕g5+ leads to forced mate. Black played five or six moves of theory, a few of his own, accepted a gambit and then managed half a dozen more.

Some players seem to lose their sense of danger when thrown into a gambit situation, and to finish this chapter we have a couple of mini miniatures in which the suddenly stormy waters induce losing blunders – in favourable positions! – from the victims.

Pratt-Korkenblatt
USA 1965

1 e4 e5 2 ♘c3 ♘f6 3 ♗c4 ♘xe4

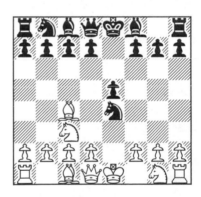

Instead of normal development Black initiates this skirmish in the centre, the point being that 4 ♘xe4 d5 more than comfortably regains the piece, while 4 ♗xf7+ ♔xf7 5 ♘xe4 sees White pay the price of the light squares for the not too inconvenient displacement of the king.

4 ♕h5 ♘d6 5 ♗b3

5 ♕xe5+ ♕e7 6 ♕xe7+ ♗xe7 7 ♗b3 ♘f5 is completely equal.

5...♘c6

Also possible is 5...♗e7, e.g. 6 ♘f3 ♘c6 7 ♘xe5 g6 8 ♘xc6 dxc6 9 ♕f3 0-0 10 0-0 ♘f5 with equality.

6 d4?!

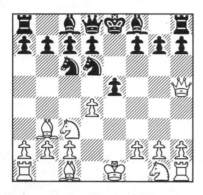

A second pawn is offered. Nowadays the established main line here is, in fact, 6 ♘b5 g6 7 ♕f3 f5 8 ♕d5 (White just won't give up on that f7-square...) 8...♕e7 9 ♘xc7+ ♔d8 10 ♘xa8, when White should eventually be able to make something of his material lead after 10...b6 11 ♘xb6 axb6. White's choice in the main game does not lead to such complex play. Nor does it promise a great deal, apart from introduce what I would have thought to be an easy to spot theme.

6...exd4

6...♘xd4 7 ♘d5 will be level after the solid 7...♘e6 8 ♕xe5 c6 etc. On the other hand, rushing to eliminate the dangerous looking bishop with 7...♘xb3? justifies White's strategy: 8 ♕xe5+ ♗e7 9 ♕xg7 ♖f8 (9...♘xa1 10 ♕xh8+ ♗f8 11 ♗h6) 10 ♗h6

---

see following diagram

White threatens 11 ♘f6+! ♗xf6 12 ♕xf8 mate, against which there is no satisfactory defence, e.g. 10...f6 11 axb3 ♘f5 12 ♕xh7 ♘xh6 13 ♕xh6.

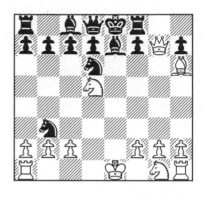

7 ♘d5

Now best is the calm 7...♗e7 8 ♗f4 0-0 9 0-0-0

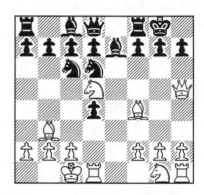

White at least has a menacing stance to show for his two pawn investment (which might be reduced to one pawn), and Black's development is far from easy. Next on the agenda is h2-h4 and ♘f3-♘g5, or ♖he1 etc. Perhaps I was too harsh earlier – this is gambit play, after all, and this is the kind of position we should enjoy. Anyway, Black was clearly not enjoying the game after 7 ♘d5, which explains why he found the startling...

7...g6??

Remember – every pawn move creates a weakness.

8 ♕e2+! ♗e7

8...♘e7 9 ♘f6 mate.

9 ♘f6+ ♔f8 10 ♗h6 mate

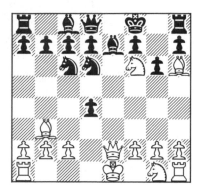

Finally an even shorter contribution that, oddly enough, is a correspondence game. That this is a miniature is an achievement in itself.

Warren-Selmann
Correspondence 1930

1 d4 ♘f6 2 c4 e5

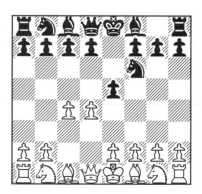

The Budapest Gambit is another tricky customer.

3 dxe5 ♘e4

3...♘g4 is the main line. The text can occasionally catch White unawares.

4 a3

A recommended reply that rules out the simplifying check.

4...d6 5 exd6?!

Taking on d6 simply accelerates Black's development. The best course involves addressing the exposed knight. Reshevsky-Bisguier, New York 1954/5 is a good example: 5 ♘f3 ♘c6 6 ♕c2! ♗f5 7 ♘c3 ♘xf2 8 ♕xf5 ♘xh1 9 e6 fxe6 10 ♕xe6+ ♕e7 11 ♕d5 h6 12 g3 g5 13 ♗g2 ♘xg3 14 hxg3 and the minor pieces gave White a clear advantage. Here 7...♘g3 8 e4 ♘xh1 9 exf5 dxe5 10 ♗e3 ♗e7 11 ♕e4 0-0 12 ♗d3 f6 13 0-0-0, Montag-Heyer, Correspondence 1995 is close to winning for White according to *NCO*.

5...♗xd6

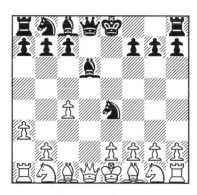

After only five moves White is already in danger of playing a futile game of catch-up, and with Black's forces so active, alarm bells should be ringing.

6 g3??

6 ♘d2 both spoils Black's party and challenges the knight.

6...♘xf2! 7 ♔xf2?

Not best, but even 7 ♕d5 will leave White an exchange down with nothing to show for it.

7...♗xg3+ 0-1

This was an incredible blunder from White considering the circumstances, although it would not be so unusual to see it happen when the clock is ticking. The 3...♘e4 line of the Budapest is often employed as a means of unsettling the opponent with the unwelcome knight, and it certainly worked here. White made life difficult for himself with 5 exd6 but then completely failed to appreciate the danger. Another curse of the gambit.